Chapter 1: Addition 1

Introducing the thousand

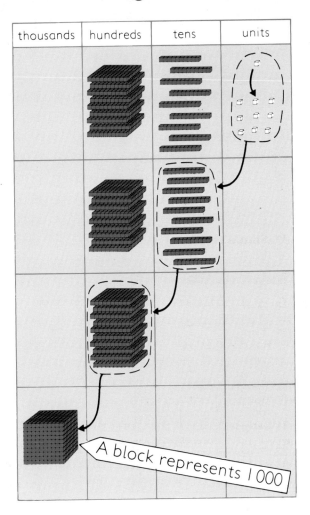

thousands	hundreds	tens	units

A block represents 1 000

I is added to 999.

10 units
are exchanged
for I ten.

This makes 10 tens.

10 tens
are exchanged
for I hundred.

This makes
10 hundreds.

10 hundreds
are exchanged
for I thousand.

1 0 0 0

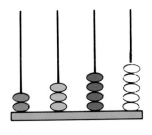

Two thousand
three hundred
and forty-five
looks like this:

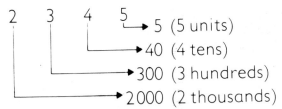

2 3 4 5 → 5 (5 units)
→ 40 (4 tens)
→ 300 (3 hundreds)
→ 2000 (2 thousands)

thousands	hundreds	tens	units

1 Here are some numbers set out in blocks, squares, longs and units or in tokens.
Draw an abacus picture and write each number in figures and in words.

a

thousands	hundreds	tens	units

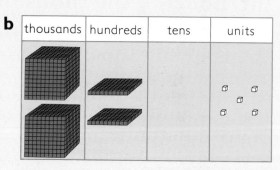

b

thousands	hundreds	tens	units

c

thousands	hundreds	tens	units

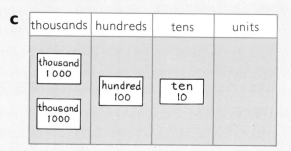

d

thousands	hundreds	tens	units

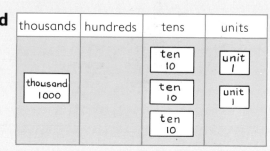

2 Copy these abacus pictures. Write the number each shows in figures and in words.

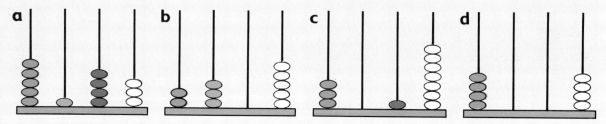

a   **b**   **c**   **d**

3 Draw abacus pictures for these and write the numbers in figures underneath.

   a Seven thousand two hundred and forty-eight.
   b Eight thousand seven hundred and eighteen.
   c One thousand and one.   **e** Six thousand and sixty.
   d Two thousand and twelve.   **f** Nineteen hundred and ninety.

4 Add 1 to each of these numbers. Draw an abacus picture of your answer and write it in words and figures.
   a 1094   **b** 2129   **c** 5039   **d** 3992   **e** 2099   **f** 999

5 Repeat question 4 but this time add 10 to each number.

Adding thousands, hundreds, tens and units

thousands	hundreds	tens	units

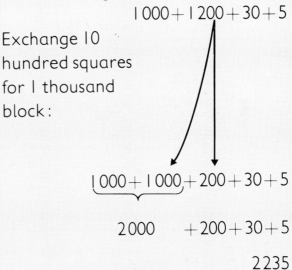

This is how the counting board is used to add 1512 and 723.

Set out 1512:

$$1000 + 500 + 10 + 2$$

and 723:

$$700 + 20 + 3$$

Add them together:

$$1000 + 1200 + 30 + 5$$

Exchange 10 hundred squares for 1 thousand block:

$$1000 + 1000 + 200 + 30 + 5$$

$$2000 \quad + 200 + 30 + 5$$

$$2235$$

1 Estimate first by rounding numbers to the nearest 1000.
(500 and below, round **down**; over 500, round **up**.)
For example, in **g** the estimate is 5000 + 1000 = 6000

Use some blocks, squares, longs and units (or tokens)

 thousand 1000 hundred 100 ten 10 unit 1

on a counting board for these:

a	1512 + 340	**c**	736 +2441	**e**	2176 +2024	**g**	4783 +1146	**i**	3927 +4846
b	2653 +1542	**d**	863 + 844	**f**	3002 +1139	**h**	1927 +2073	**j**	345 + 656

4

We can add 2372 and 1416 like this:

$$
\begin{array}{r}
2372 \\
+1416 \\
\hline
3788
\end{array}
\longrightarrow
\begin{array}{l}
2000+300+70+2 \\
1000+400+10+6 \\
\hline
3000+700+80+8
\end{array}
$$

1 Set these out the same way, estimate to the nearest 1000 first.

a $\begin{array}{r}2174\\+3723\\\hline\end{array}$	**b** $\begin{array}{r}718\\+2131\\\hline\end{array}$	**c** $\begin{array}{r}1357\\+8642\\\hline\end{array}$	**d** $\begin{array}{r}5665\\+2024\\\hline\end{array}$

$$
\begin{array}{ll}
1463 \longrightarrow & 1000 \quad + \quad 400 \quad + \quad 60 \quad + \quad 3 \\
+3819 \longrightarrow & 3000 \quad + \quad 800 \quad + \quad 10 \quad + \quad 9 \\
\hline
& 4000 \quad + \quad 1200 \quad + \quad 70 \quad + \quad 12 \\
& 4000+1000+200 \quad + \quad 70+10 \quad + \quad 2 \\
\hline
5282 \longleftarrow \quad & 5000 \quad +200 \quad + \quad 80 \quad + \quad 2
\end{array}
$$

2 Set these out in the same way, estimate to the nearest 1000 first.

a $\begin{array}{r}1575\\+2319\\\hline\end{array}$	**b** $\begin{array}{r}3424\\+\ 765\\\hline\end{array}$	**c** $\begin{array}{r}5386\\+1819\\\hline\end{array}$	**d** $\begin{array}{r}4388\\+1831\\\hline\end{array}$

Horizontal layout

$$
\begin{array}{ll}
2378 \longrightarrow & 2000+300+ 70+ 8 \\
+4149 \longrightarrow & 4000+100+ 40+ 9 \\
\hline
& 6000+400+110+17 \\
\\
6527 \longleftarrow & 6000+500+20+7
\end{array}
$$

Vertical layout

$$
\begin{array}{r}
2378 \\
+4149 \\
\hline
17 \\
110 \\
400 \\
6000 \\
\hline
6527
\end{array}
\qquad
\begin{array}{l}
(8+9) \\
(70+40) \\
(300+100) \\
(2000+4000)
\end{array}
$$

3 Set these out vertically, estimate to the nearest 1000 first.

a $\begin{array}{r}1675\\+3279\\\hline\end{array}$	**b** $\begin{array}{r}4306\\+1274\\\hline\end{array}$	**c** $\begin{array}{r}3675\\+\ 895\\\hline\end{array}$	**d** $\begin{array}{r}1362\\+2028\\\hline\end{array}$	**e** $\begin{array}{r}1696\\+2604\\\hline\end{array}$

Here is an even shorter way of recording addition.

6+9 = 15 → 1 ten and 5 units
Write 5 in the 'units' column of answer
and 1 below in 'tens' column

```
 2536
+4829
    5
─────
  1
```

30+20+10 = 60 → 6 tens
Write 6 in the 'tens' column of answer.

```
 2536
+4829
   65
─────
  1
```

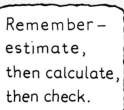

Remember –
estimate,
then calculate,
then check.

500+800 = 1 300 → 1 thousand and 3 hundreds
Write three in 'hundreds' column of answer and
1 below in 'thousands' column.

```
 2536
+4829
  365
─────
 1  1
```

2000+4000+1 000 = 7000
Write 7 in 'thousands' column.

```
 2536
+4829
 7365
─────
 1  1
```

1 Use the shorter way of recording for these:

a	c	e	g	i
1465	5428	1978	72	69
+2217	+1742	+2978	8	1701
			+619	+2150

b	d	f	h	j
3291	4536	1235	1037	1549
+1476	+3464	312	337	2439
		+1251	+ 37	+3076

2

Be sure to write
figures in the
correct columns.

a 7007+707+77
b 1732+6+109
c 39+762+440+14
d 2106+210+106+26

1 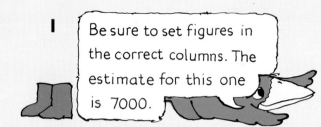 Be sure to set figures in the correct columns. The estimate for this one is 7000.

   a Add six thousand and six,   6006
        six hundred and sixteen   616
        and sixty-six   +   66
                                    ——

   b Add five thousand five hundred and five to five thousand and fifteen.

   c Find the total of eight thousand and eighty-eight, eighteen and eight hundred and eight.

2 Write down the answers to:
   a 1 more than 1999.   **b** 200 less than 2000.
   c 100 more than 1955.
   d Find the total of your answers to **a**, **b** and **c**.

3 If a man is born in 1969 and lives for 75 years, in which year will he die?

4 Queen Victoria came to the throne in 1837 and reigned for 64 years, in which year did she die?

5 An odometer shows the number of kilometres a car has travelled.

   a A man buys a car which shows |4|3|7|6| on the odometer. In one week he travels 828 kilometres; what does the odometer show now?

   b In the second week, he travels another 1052 kilometres, what does the odometer show now?

   c How many kilometres did he travel in the two weeks?

6 Add together:

   a numbers in the circles
   b numbers in the squares
   c numbers in the triangles
   d the odd numbers
   e the even numbers

 923   2347   1586
1024   1705   466

   f Check that the sum of the answers **a**, **b** and **c** equals the sum of answers **d** and **e**.

Chapter 2: Shape 1

Angles-degree measurement

Using very simple instruments the Babylonians, before 4 000 B.C., had the mistaken idea that the Sun travelled round the Earth and that it took only 360 days. Because of this they divided a complete turn into 360 parts and called each part **a degree (written as 1°).**

One complete turn = 360°.
Half a complete turn = 180°.
A quarter of a complete turn or one right-angle = 90°.

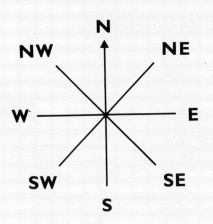

1 The angle between N and E measured in a clockwise direction is a right angle. How many degrees is it?

2 The angle between N and NE measured in a clockwise direction is half a right angle. How many degrees is it?

3 The angle between N and SW measured in an anti-clockwise direction is $1\frac{1}{2}$ right angles. How many degrees is it?

4 Copy and complete

I start facing	I turn through	Direction	I finish facing
North	180°	Clockwise	
South	90°	Anti-clockwise	
East	360°	Clockwise	
West	135°	Clockwise	
North East	225°		South
South West		Clockwise	South East
North West	270°		North East
South East		Clockwise	North
South East	315°		South
South East		Anti-clockwise	West

1 How many degrees does the minute hand of a clock turn through in one hour?

2 How long does it take the hour hand to turn through 360°?

3 How many degrees does the minute hand turn through in a quarter of an hour?

4 How many degrees does the minute hand turn through in 5 minutes?

5 In three hours the hour hand turns through how many degrees?

6 How many degrees does the hour hand turn through in one hour?

7 Copy and complete:

Hand of clock	From	To	Turns through (degrees)
hour hand	1	4	
minute hand	3	6	
minute hand	2	8	
hour hand	5	11	
minute hand	4	8	
hour hand	6	11	
minute hand	11	4	
hour hand	10	5	

Describing angles

A **right angle** = 90°

An **acute angle** is less than a right angle so an acute angle is less than 90°.

An **obtuse angle** is more than one right angle but less than two right angles so an obtuse angle is more than 90° but less than 180°.

A **reflex angle** is more than 180°.

8 List these angles and say whether they are acute, obtuse or reflex.

a 36°   c 79°   e 163°   g 210°   i 34°   k 21°

b 141°   d 188°   f 17°   h 96°   j 175°   l 300°

Angles of a triangle

1 Draw any triangle on
a piece of paper.
Mark the angles **A**, **B** and **C**
as in the diagram.

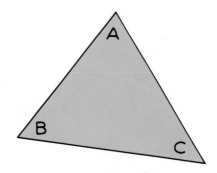

Tear off each angle as shown:

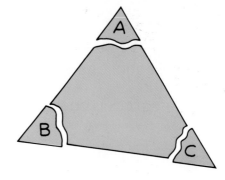

Stick the three angles in
your book like this:

Together they make 180° or
two right angles.

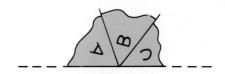

> The angles of a triangle add up to 180°.

2 For each triangle calculate the size of the unmarked angle:

a 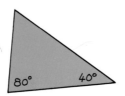 70° 60°

b 80° 40°

c 55° 65°

d 100° 30°

e 85° 35°

f 54° 67°

Angles in special triangles

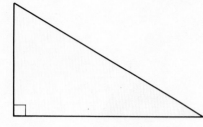

A triangle with one angle of 90° is called a **right-angled triangle.** The right angle is often marked as in the diagram.

A triangle with its three sides equal is called an **equilateral triangle**. It also has three equal angles.

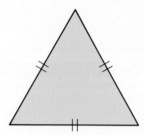

1 How many degrees is each angle?

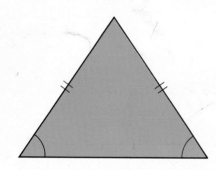

A triangle with two equal sides is an **isosceles triangle**. It has two equal angles.

2 If one of the equal angles of an isosceles triangle is 55°, what are the sizes of the other two angles in the triangle?

Draw a square and the diagonal shown in the diagram.

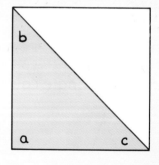

3 How many degrees is the angle marked **a**?

4 How many is the angle marked **b**?

5 How many is the angle marked **c**?

6 Describe the triangle shaded in the diagram in two different ways.

7 For each triangle, calculate the size of the angles marked with letters.

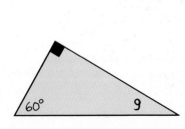
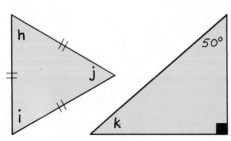
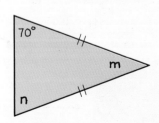

Chapter 3: Subtraction 1

Splitting thousands

A **block** represents 1000. It can be exchanged for 10 **squares** (ten hundreds)
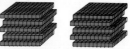

1 thousand token | thousand 1000 | is worth | 10 hundred tokens
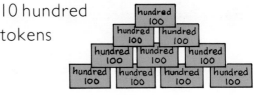

For 3245 − 1419
Set out 3245 as
$3(1000)+2(100)+4(10)+5(1)$.

There are not enough units and not enough hundreds to take away.
$1(1000)+4(100)+1(10)+9(1)$.

Exchange a 1000 block for ten 100 squares and a 10 rod for ten units, so that there are
$2(1000)+12(100)+3(10)+15(1)$

thousands	hundreds	tens	units

Now you can take away 1419 leaving the answer: 1826.

thousands	hundreds	tens	units

Record like this:
Estimate: $3000 - 1000 = 2000$

$$
\begin{array}{l}
3245 \longrightarrow (3000+200+40+5) \longrightarrow (2000+1200+30+15)\\
-1419 \longrightarrow -(1000+400+10+9) \longrightarrow -(1000+\ 400+10+\ 9)\\
\overline{\ 1826} \longleftarrow \overline{(1000+\ 800+20+\ 6)}
\end{array}
$$

Remember—estimate, calculate, check.

1 Use blocks, squares, longs and units or token cards for these:
a $2174 - 851$ **b** $3561 - 1825$ **c** $1632 - 856$ **d** $4000 - 2345$

2 Copy and complete to show the exchange in question **d**.
$$4000 = \Box\,(1000) + \Box\,(100) + \Box\,(10) + \Box\,(1)$$

This is how $3245 - 1419$ is set out the short way:

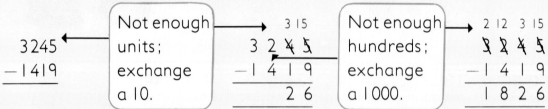

$$
\begin{array}{r}
3245 \\
-1419 \\
\hline
\end{array}
\quad
\text{Not enough units; exchange a 10.}
\quad
\begin{array}{r}
{}^{3\ 15}\\
3\,2\,\cancel{4}\,\cancel{5} \\
-1\,4\,1\,9 \\
\hline
2\,6 \\
\end{array}
\quad
\text{Not enough hundreds; exchange a 1000.}
\quad
\begin{array}{r}
{}^{2\ 12\ \ 3\ 15}\\
\cancel{3}\,\cancel{2}\,\cancel{4}\,\cancel{5} \\
-1\,4\,1\,9 \\
\hline
1\,8\,2\,6 \\
\end{array}
$$

$\overset{2\ 12\ \ 3\ 15}{\cancel{3}\,\cancel{2}\,\cancel{4}\,\cancel{5}}$ shows that $3(1000) + 2(100) + 4(10) + 5(1)$
were exchanged for $2(1000) + 12(100) + 3(10) + 15(1)$

3 Try these. Some have been started for you.

a
$$
\begin{array}{r}
{}^{1\ \ 13}\\
\cancel{2}\,\cancel{3}\,4\,0 \\
-1\,8\,2\,0 \\
\hline
\end{array}
$$

b
$$
\begin{array}{r}
{}^{7\ 11\ 15}\\
4\,\cancel{8}\,\cancel{2}\,\cancel{5} \\
-2\,5\,3\,7 \\
\hline
\end{array}
$$

c
$$
\begin{array}{r}
{}^{9\ 14\ 10}\\
\cancel{1}\,\cancel{0}\,\cancel{5}\,\cancel{0} \\
-\ \ 9\,7\,9 \\
\hline
\end{array}
$$

d
$$
\begin{array}{r}
{}^{7\ 9\ 9\ 10}\\
\cancel{8}\,\cancel{0}\,\cancel{0}\,\cancel{0} \\
-6\,0\,5\,2 \\
\hline
\end{array}
$$

e
$$
\begin{array}{r}
5000 \\
-2345 \\
\hline
\end{array}
$$

f
$$
\begin{array}{r}
4225 \\
-2537 \\
\hline
\end{array}
$$

g
$$
\begin{array}{r}
3372 \\
-1493 \\
\hline
\end{array}
$$

h
$$
\begin{array}{r}
7120 \\
-2389 \\
\hline
\end{array}
$$

i
$$
\begin{array}{r}
4321 \\
-1234 \\
\hline
\end{array}
$$

j
$$
\begin{array}{r}
5104 \\
-3826 \\
\hline
\end{array}
$$

4 The graph shows the points scored by four teams.

Green team's score	1225
Red team's score	− 950
Difference	275

Find the difference between the scores of:
a The Blue and Yellow teams
b The Yellow and Red teams
c The Green and Yellow teams
d The Green and Blue teams

5 How much greater is the highest than the lowest score?

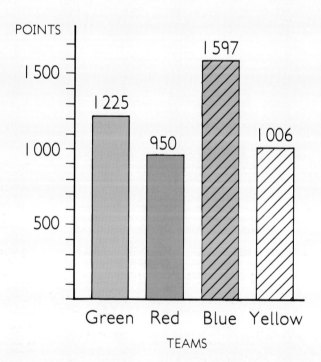

How many points must Red win to equal Green's score?
The question is asking:

$$950 \text{ and how many make } 1\,225?$$
$$\text{or } 950 + \boxed{} = 1\,225$$

To find the **difference** between 950 and 1 225 we can
either subtract   or add
$1\,225 - 950 = \boxed{}$ $950 + \boxed{} = 1\,225$

Difference problems can be
solved by 'making up' the
smaller to the larger number
using a zig-zag layout.

For example, $1\,518 + \boxed{1\,627} = 3\,145$

or $3\,145 - 1\,518 = \boxed{1\,627}$

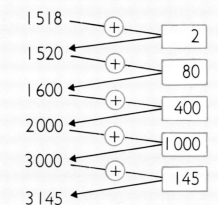

Total difference $\boxed{1\,627}$

1 Rewrite each sentence as an addition problem, then use the zig-zag layout to find the difference. The first one is done for you.

a $167 - 128 = \square$ **c** $2035 - 1679 = \square$ **e** $6371 - 4298 = \square$
b $1410 - 1286 = \square$ **d** $4203 - 2345 = \square$ **f** $8009 - 5290 = \square$

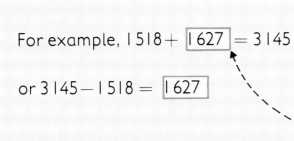

a $128 + \boxed{} = 167$

$128 + \boxed{39} = 167$

or $167 - 128 \quad = 39$

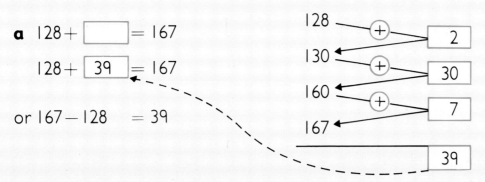

2 Estimate first, then try doing these 'in your head'
using the 'making up' method.
Write down the answers and then check by a written method.

a $28 + \square = 60$ **c** $790 + \square = 1\,000$ **e** $1784 + \square = 2000$
b $86 + \square = 131$ **d** $168 + \square = 501$ **f** $1890 + \square = 3224$

1 Work out numbers
to go in the empty frames
lettered **a, b, c, d, e, f** and **g**.

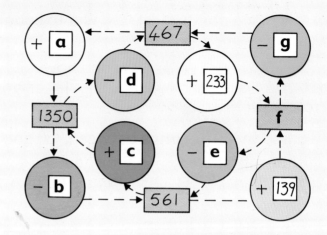

2 So far Anne has read 768 pages
of a book with 1 025 pages in it.
How many more pages must
she read to finish the book?

3 How much greater is the capacity of a Cortina (1 593 cm³) than
a Mini (998 cm³)?

4 Station

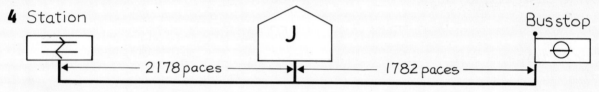

John paces the distances from his house to the station and,
in the opposite direction, to the bus stop.
   a How much farther is the station than the bus stop from his house?
   b How many paces is it from the station to the bus stop?

5 Here are the dates of some
Royal families who have
ruled England.

Normans	1066 to 1154
Plantagenets	1154 to 1485
Tudors	1485 to 1603
House of Hanover	1714 to 1901

   a Which family ruled the longest?
   b Which family ruled the shortest time?
   c How many more years did the Plantagenets rule than the Tudors?
   d How many years shorter was Norman rule than
      the House of Hanover's rule?

6 At the start of a journey the odometer shows 7 7 8 6 km

and 8 0 2 5 km at the end. How long was the journey?

7 What is the difference in price of a car costing £6 582 and a caravan
costing £3 825.

Chapter 4: Area 1

Areas and perimeters

Use a ruler to copy these rectangles
on to squared centimetre paper.

Rectangle A has 6 cm² in a row
and 4 rows.
$6 \times 4 = 24$
so area of A = 24 cm²

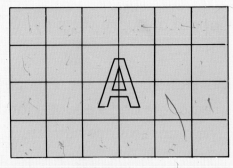

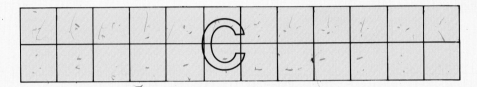

1 Copy the table and fill in the first 3 columns.

	Length in centimetres	Breadth in centimetres	Area in square centimetres	Perimeter in centimetres
A	6cm	4cm	24cm²	. . . . . .cm
B				
C				

Perimeter is the distance around a shape.
Do you remember a quick way to work out the perimeters of rectangles?
Fill in the 4th column of your table.

2 Write a sentence about the areas and perimeters of **A**, **B** and **C**.

3 Draw these on cm-squared paper and answer the questions.
  a Rectangle **D** is 7cm long, 3cm wide. Find its area and perimeter.
  b Rectangle **E** is 9cm long, 1cm wide. Find its area and perimeter.
  c The area of rectangle **F** is 16cm² and it is 8cm long.
     Find its breadth and perimeter.
  d Square **G** has a perimeter of 20cm. Find its area.

4 Write a sentence about the areas and perimeters of **D**, **E**, **F** and **G**.

Making shapes

Cut out a square 10cm by 10cm from card.

Mark and cut out the 5 shapes:
1 rectangle and 4 equal triangles.
(The diagrams are half size.)

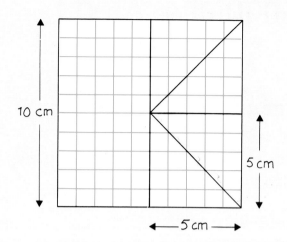

10 cm

5 cm

←—5 cm—→

1 Use all five pieces
without overlapping
to make each shape
and copy it onto
1 cm² paper.

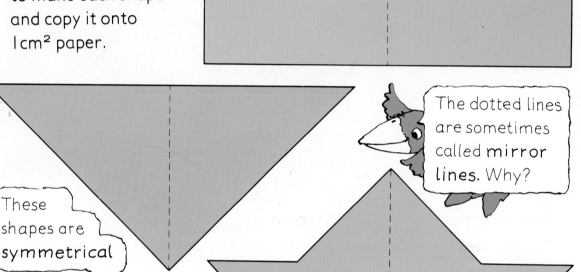

The dotted lines
are sometimes
called **mirror
lines**. Why?

These
shapes are
symmetrical

They each
have at least one
axis of symmetry.

2 a What is the area of each shape in question 1?
  b Measure and record the perimeter of each shape.
  c Write a sentence about the area and perimeters.

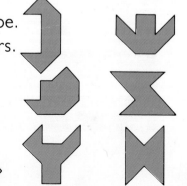

3 Make some more shapes with the 5 pieces.
Record them on 1 cm² squared paper.
Mark in any axes of symmetry.
Measure and record the perimeters.

Larger areas

On cm² paper draw a square with sides 10cm long.

Carefully cut out the square—you will need it later.

Copy the sentence about the area on to your square.

The area of this square is 100 square centimetres

or

1 square decimetre

100 cm² = 1 dm²

10 cm

10cm

1 Estimate how many of your squares would be needed to cover:
  a your desk top   **c** a flagstone in the playground
  b the classroom door   **d** a classroom window pane

The best way to estimate is to try to imagine how many of your squares would fit into a row and how many rows.

For example: 8 in a row; 4 rows
          8 × 4 = 32

Estimate 32dm²
    or 3200cm²

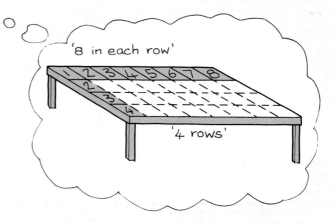

'8 in each row'

'4 rows'

2 Use your square cut-out to check how accurate your estimates were for question **1**.
    Record the areas   **a** in square decimetres (dm²) and
                        b in square centimetres (cm²).

The diagrams of two table tops had to be drawn smaller than they really are in order to fit them on this page.

They are drawn to **scale**.

1cm represents 10cm (or 1dm)
1cm² represents 100cm² (or 1dm²)

picnic table

coffee table

1 **a** How many of your 1dm² squares are needed to cover each table?
   b What is the area of each table in cm²?
   c Which table has the greater area and by how many cm²?
   d What is the perimeter of each table in cm?
   e Write a sentence about the areas
      and perimeters of the tables.

2 Copy each shape on 1cm² paper
   using the **scale**.
   1cm represents 10cm (1dm)
   1cm² represents 100cm² (1dm²)

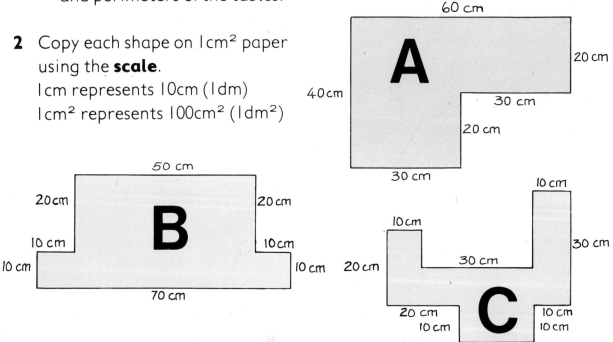

Copy and complete this table.

Shape	Number of dm² to cover	Area in cm²	Perimeter in cm
A			
B			
C			

1 Make a square metre by
using a metre rule and
sheets of newspaper;
or using 4 metre rules;
or pegging out string.
(How long will the string
be?)

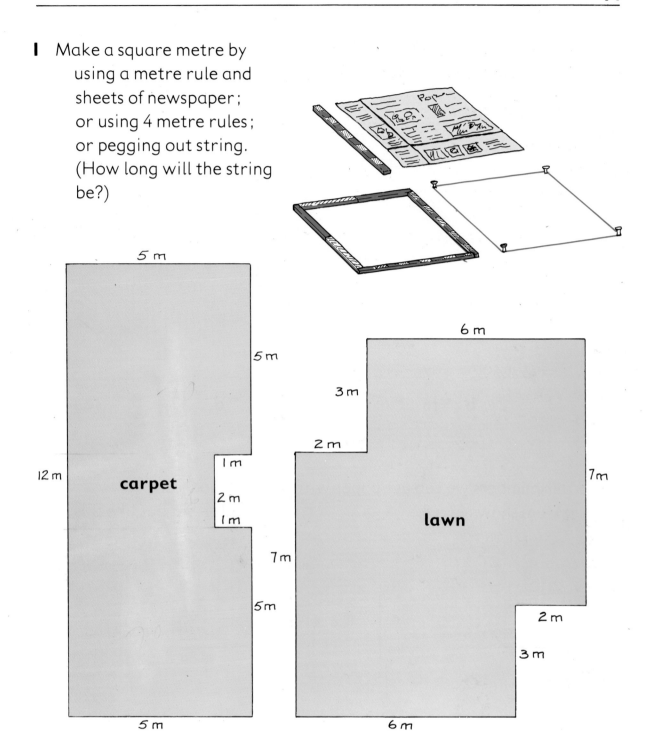

5 m

5 m

12 m   **carpet**

1 m

2 m

1 m

5 m

6 m

3 m

2 m

7 m

lawn

7 m

5 m

2 m

3 m

6 m

2 **a** Find the area and perimeter of the carpet and of the lawn.
    Write a sentence about your results.
  b What is the cost of the carpet at £8 per m²?
  c If it takes 5 minutes to mow 10m², could you mow the lawn
    in under half an hour?
  d How long will it take to trim the edge (perimeter) of the lawn
    if you can trim 2 metres in a minute?

Chapter 5: Multiplication 1

This diagram shows 17×6.   It is set out like this:

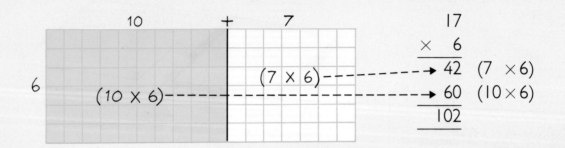

I Do these the same way:

a 13	**b** 16	**c** 18	**d** 17	**e** 19
× 4	× 7	× 6	× 9	× 8

For larger numbers we can use paper with smaller squares.
This diagram shows 23×8.   It is set out like this:

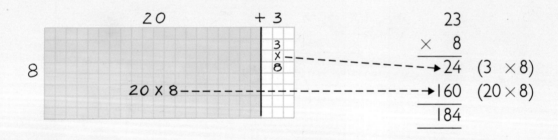

2 Do these in the same way. Draw a diagram and then set them out.

a 24	**c** 28	**e** 34	**g** 57	**i** 59
× 3	× 6	× 8	× 5	× 7
b 31	**d** 37	**f** 46	**h** 48	**j** 47
× 4	× 7	× 9	× 8	× 6

Remember: estimate, calculate, check.

3 Set these out and complete them without using a diagram.

a 43	**b** 37	**c** 63	**d** 54	**e** 76
× 6	× 8	× 7	× 9	× 5

Flow charts

Multiplication can be set out like this:

27 × 7

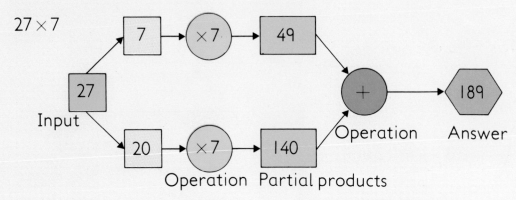

Here is another example

36 × 9

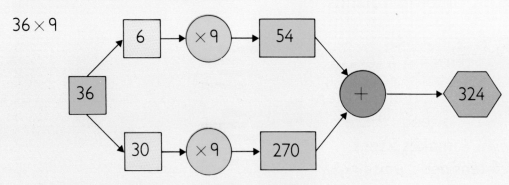

1 Copy and complete these diagrams

a 58 × 5

b 75 × 9

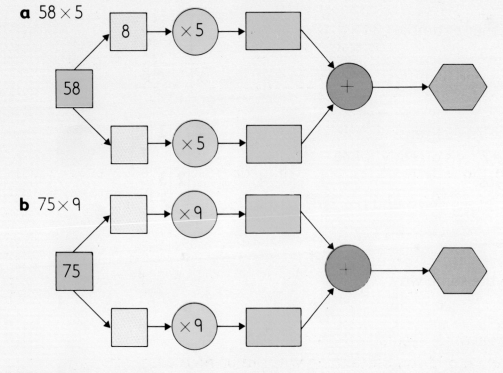

2 Do these in the same way, drawing your own diagram for each.
a 73 × 6   **b** 89 × 8   **c** 96 × 7   **d** 68 × 8

A shorter way to multiply

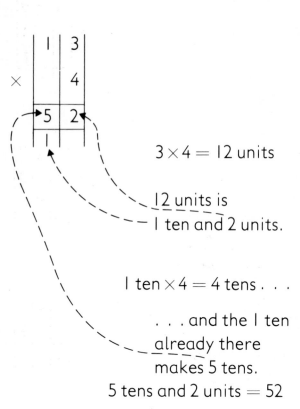

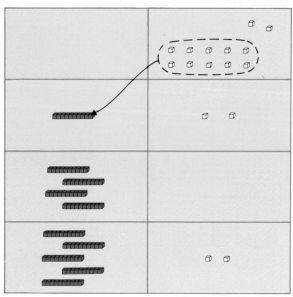

$3 \times 4 = 12$ units

12 units is
1 ten and 2 units.

1 ten $\times 4 = 4$ tens . . .

. . . and the 1 ten
already there
makes 5 tens.
5 tens and 2 units $= 52$

Here is another example: 34×7
$4 \times 7 = 28$
that is 2 tens and 8 units.

3 tens $\times 7 = 21$ tens. . .
. . . and the 2 tens already there
makes 23 tens.
2 hundreds 3 tens and 8 units $= 238$.

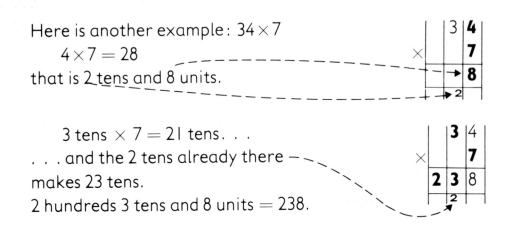

1 Do these the same way

a	27	**c**	38	**e**	37	**g**	63	**i**	83
	× 3		× 5		× 4		× 8		× 7
b	34	**d**	43	**f**	57	**h**	49	**j**	92
	× 6		× 6		× 7		× 6		× 9

Multiplying hundreds, tens and units

hundreds	tens	units

7 units × 3 = 21 units

or 2 tens and 1 unit.

×3

4 tens × 3 = 12 tens
and 2 tens below make
14 tens.

or 1 hundred and 4 tens
1 hundred × 3 = 3 hundreds
and 1 hundred below
makes 4 hundreds.

Here is another example: 264 × 6

4 units × 6 = 24 units
that is, 2 tens and 4 units.
6 tens × 6 = 36 tens . . .
. . and the 2 tens below make
38 tens or 3 hundreds and 8 tens
2 hundreds × 6 = 12 hundreds . . .
. . and the 3 hundreds below make
15 hundreds or 1 thousand 5 hundreds.

Estimate: 200 × 6 = 1200, 300 × 6 = 1800
so answer will be between 1200 and 1800.

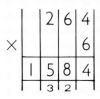

1 Do these the same way:

a	134	**c**	176	**e**	645	**g**	483
	× 3		× 4		× 8		× 7
b	225	**d**	328	**f**	396	**h**	627
	× 5		× 6		× 9		× 9

1 **a** If there are 16 crayons in a packet, how many will there be in 7 packets?

b How many buttons will be needed for 9 coats if each coat has 14 buttons on it?

c How much will 18 packets of crisps cost if each costs 8p?

d A packet contains 15 biscuits.
How many biscuits will there be in 6 packets?

e If my newspaper has 24 pages, how many pages will there be in 6 newspapers?

f A coach has seats for 37 children.
How many children can travel in 8 coaches?

g A carton holds two dozen boxes of soap.
How many boxes of soap will there be in 9 cartons.

h Lamp posts are placed 75 metres apart along a main road.
How far is it from the first lamp to the ninth lamp?
Warning—look at the diagram.

i There are 36 desks in each classroom of a school which has 9 classrooms. How many desks are there altogether?

j A bag of sweets costs 16p. How much will 15 bags cost?
(Give your answer first in pence then in £s.)

k If a ribbon is 18cm long, how far will 17 ribbons reach if they are put end to end?

l If there are 16 rows of tiles in the hall and each row has 18 tiles in it, how many tiles are there altogether?

m A bottle of perfume holds 18 millilitres.
How much perfume will 14 bottles contain?

Chapter 6 : Volume and Capacity

A **prism** can be thought of as a solid shape which could be cut into 'slices' or layers, all the same shape and size.

Rectangular prism
or cuboid

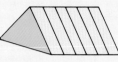

Triangular
prism

Hexagonal
prism

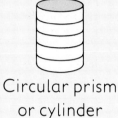

Circular prism
or cylinder

1 Which of these shapes are prisms?
Make a list, name and draw the shape
of each 'slice' or layer like this :

Prism	Shape of 'slice'
B	square ☐

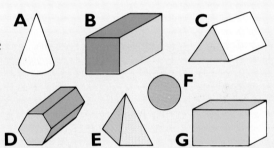

2 The **volume** of a prism is the amount of space it takes up.
Find the volumes of these rectangular prisms by counting
how many cubic centimetres (cm³) are used to make each one :

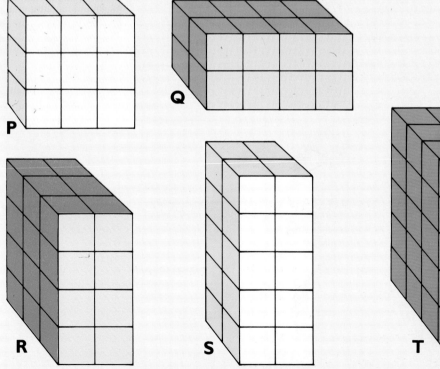

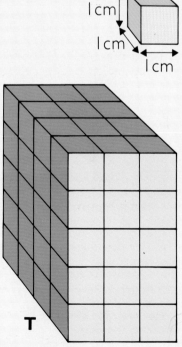

There is a quicker way to work
out the volume of a cuboid.

This cuboid looks like a sliced
loaf. It has 5 slices or
layers each 1cm thick.

The end slice contains
3 rows of 4 cubes,
that is 12cm³.

There are 5 slices or layers
with 12cm³ in each so
the volume is 12cm³ × 5 = 60cm³

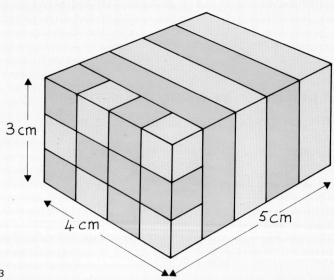

Volume of cuboid = | Number of cm³ in one layer | × | Number of layers |

I Use centimetre cubes to make and find the volume of each
of these cuboids:

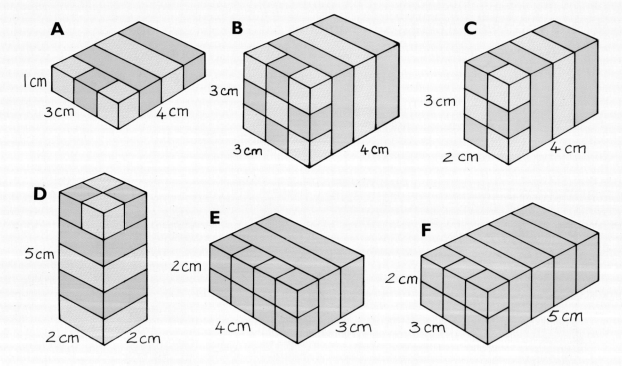

2 What do you notice about cuboids **C** and **E**?
Find other ways of making cuboids with the same volumes
as **A**, **B**, **D** and **F**.
In each case record how many cm³ in one layer and how many layers.

If we know the lengths of the edges of a cuboid we can find its volume without counting any cubes at all.

The area of the front face (the 'slice area') is 6 square centimetres.
Multiply this by the length to find the volume.

$6cm^2 \times 4cm = 24cm^3$

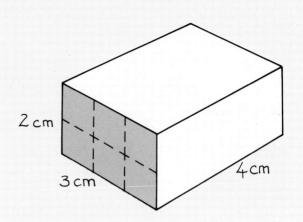

The correct name for the 'slice area' is the **area of cross-section**.
So the volume of a cuboid = area of cross section × length.

I Copy and complete the table for the volume of these cuboids.

Cuboid letter	Area of cross-section	Length	Volume
A	. . . . . . cm²	. . . cm	. . . cm³
B			

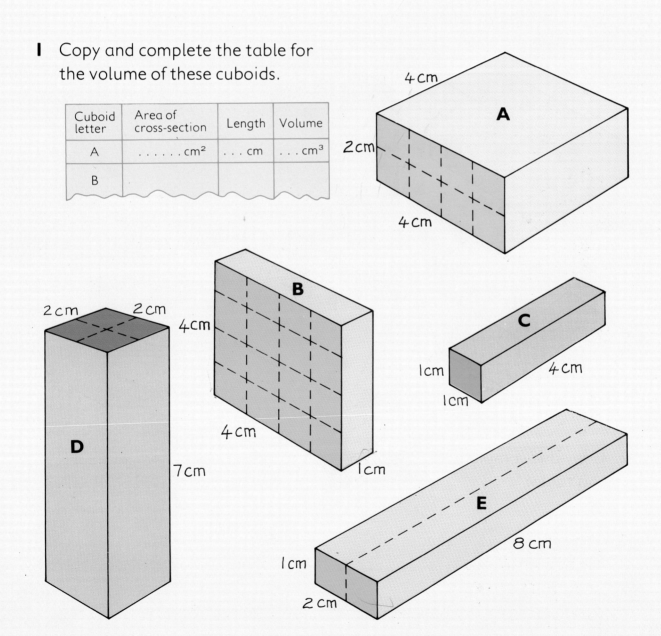

Volume = area of cross section × length works for all prisms.

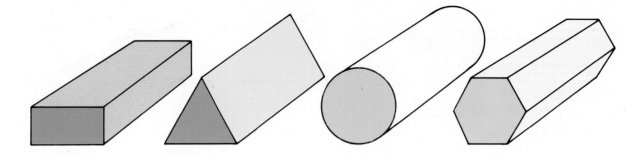

The area of cross-section of each of these prisms is 2cm² and each is 3cm long. The volume of each prism is 2cm² × 3cm = 6cm³.

1 Work out the volume of these prisms. The area of cross-section is shown on the end face.

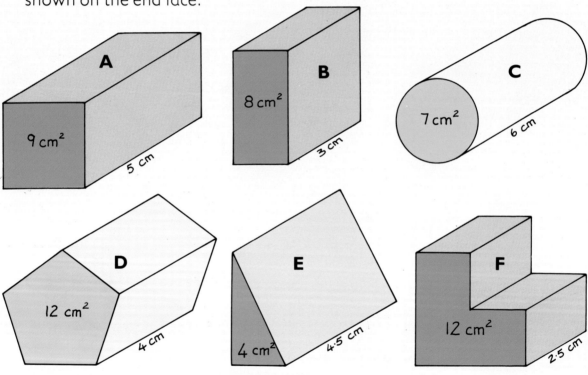

2 Copy and complete this table:

Area of end face square units	Length of prism length units	Volume of prism cubic units
15cm²	6cm	. . . . .cm³
22cm²	9cm	. . . . .cm³
100cm²	. . . . cm	1000cm³
. . . . .cm²	9cm	108cm³
6cm²	1·50m	. . . . .cm³

I For each prism, first find the area of cross-section (shaded) in cm² then work out the volume in cm³.

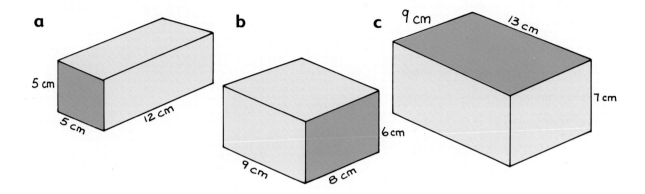

a   b   c   9 cm   13 cm

5 cm   5 cm   12 cm   9 cm   8 cm   6 cm   7 cm

The amount of space **inside** a hollow container is called
its **internal volume** or **capacity**.
The capacity of a container is how much it will hold.
Many containers are shaped like prisms:

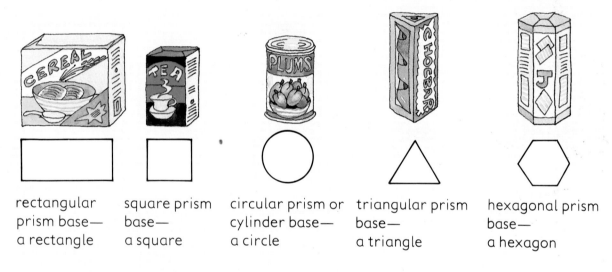

rectangular
prism base—
a rectangle

square prism
base—
a square

circular prism or
cylinder base—
a circle

triangular prism
base—
a triangle

hexagonal prism
base—
a hexagon

If the base of a prism is its cross-section, then the internal volume or
capacity = base area × height.

2 Make a collection of containers and
sort them out into those that are prisms
and those that are not prisms.

3 Try to work out a way to find the approximate
internal volume or capacity of a container
which is a prism without opening it.

If a container is made from **thin** cardboard or metal, its **approximate capacity** can be worked out from outside measurements.

For some prisms you may have to find the area of cross-section by drawing round the base on centimetre-squared paper and counting the squares.

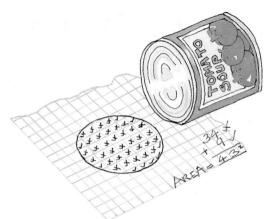

Whole squares (X)   34
Half or more (✓)   + 9
Area ≃   43cm²

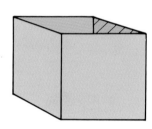

This hollow decimetre cube has a capacity of 1000cm³ or 1 litre.
Liquids are usually measured in litres or millilitres.
1000ml = 1 litre.
1ml of liquid takes up 1cm³ of space.

1 What is the base area of this fish tank in cm²?

2 What is the fish tank's capacity
    a in cm³?
    b in litres?

3 If the water in the tank is 11cm deep, what is the volume of water
    a in cm³? **b** in litres?

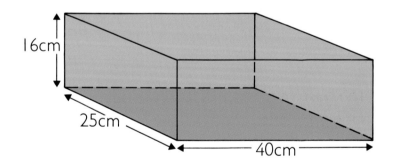

16cm
25cm
40cm

4 If another 2 litres of water is poured in, what will the new depth be?

5 Work out the measurements for other hollow cuboids which hold 1 litre, for example, 4cm × 10cm × 25cm.

Chapter 7: Division 1

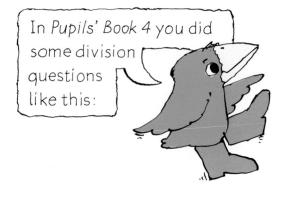

In *Pupils' Book 4* you did some division questions like this:

```
        14 r 1
  4 ) 57
     -40 | 10 (4)
       17
     -16 |  4 (4)
        1 | 14 (4)
```

1 Do these the same way:

a $73 \div 5$ **c** $41 \div 3$ **e** $68 \div 6$ **g** $75 \div 6$
b $81 \div 7$ **d** $93 \div 8$ **f** $53 \div 4$ **h** $93 \div 7$

To divide larger numbers, we need to remember how to multiply by 10. The digits move one column to the left and the units space is filled with a zero.

$$7 \times 10 = 70$$

$$27 \times 10 = 270$$

2 Copy and complete these:

a $9 \times 10 =$ **c** $14 \times 10 =$ **e** $23 \times 10 =$ **g** $48 \times 10 =$
b $11 \times 10 =$ **d** $19 \times 10 =$ **f** $34 \times 10 =$ **h** $73 \times 10 =$

Multiplication by a multiple of 10 (20, 30, 40, 50 . . .) is done in two steps like this:

$7 \times 30 = 7 \times 3 \times 10$ ← 1st step
$= 21 \times 10$ ← 2nd step
$= \underline{210}$

$56 \times 40 = 56 \times 4 \times 10$ ← 1st step
$= 224 \times 10$ ← 2nd step
$= \underline{2240}$

3 Copy and complete these:

a $9 \times 20 =$ **c** $12 \times 60 =$ **e** $34 \times 30 =$ **g** $68 \times 70 =$
b $8 \times 40 =$ **d** $27 \times 50 =$ **f** $53 \times 80 =$ **h** $79 \times 90 =$

Look at this example: 3) 73

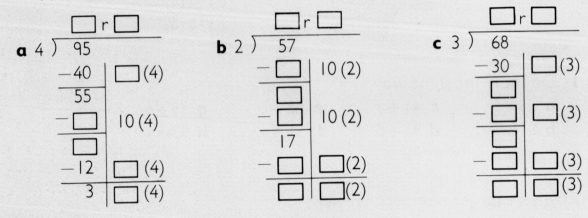

3) 73
−30 | 10 (3)
43

When 10 lots of 3 are subtracted --- there are so many left that 10 more lots of 3 can be taken away. ---

3) 73
−30 | 10 (3)
43
−30 | 10 (3)
13

Now four lots of 3 can be subtracted.

24 r 1
3) 73
−30 | 10 (3)
43
−30 | 10 (3)
13
−12 | 4 (3)
1 | 24 (3)

1 Copy and complete these:

a 4) 95   □ r □
−40 | □ (4)
55
−□ | 10 (4)
□
−12 | □ (4)
3 | □ (4)

b 2) 57   □ r □
−□ | 10 (2)
□
−□ | 10 (2)
17
−□ | □ (2)
□ | □ (2)

c 3) 68   □ r □
−30 | □ (3)
□
−□ | □ (3)
□
−□ | □ (3)
□ | □ (3)

Division of three digit numbers

The estimate for 346 ÷ 9:
9 × 30 = 270   9 × 40 = 360.
346 is between 270 and 360 so the answer will be between 30 and 40.

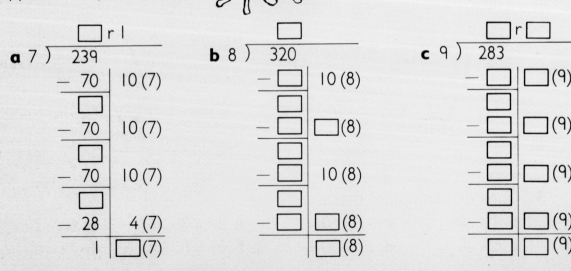

38 r 4
9) 346
− 90 | 10 (9)
256
− 90 | 10 (9)
166
− 90 | 10 (9)
76
− 72 | 8 (9)
4 | 38 (9)

2 Copy and complete these:

a 7) 239   □ r 1
− 70 | 10 (7)
□
− 70 | 10 (7)
□
− 70 | 10 (7)
□
− 28 | 4 (7)
1 | □ (7)

b 8) 320   □
−□ | 10 (8)
□
−□ | □ (8)
□
−□ | 10 (8)
□
−□ | □ (8)
□ | □ (8)

c 9) 283   □ r □
−□ | □ (9)
□
−□ | □ (9)
□
−□ | □ (9)
−□ | □ (9)
□ | □ (9)

1 Do these, setting them out in the same way:

Remember to estimate first. In **a**, $4 \times 30 = 120$
and 127 is just over 120, so the answer will be just over 30.

a $127 \div 4$ **c** $120 \div 3$ **e** $192 \div 6$ **g** $273 \div 7$

b $193 \div 5$ **d** $229 \div 7$ **f** $259 \div 8$ **h** $345 \div 9$

i 204 eggs are to be packed into boxes of 6.
How many boxes are needed?

j How many weeks are there in 252 days?

Shorter layout

Here is a shorter method
for division:

```
        36 r 3
   9 ) 327
     -270 | 30 (9)
       57 |
     - 54 |  6 (9)
        3 | 36 (9)
```

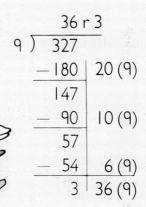

If we don't subtract all the lots of 10 together it doesn't matter. The longer way still works.

```
        36 r 3
   9 ) 327
     -180 | 20 (9)
      147 |
     - 90 | 10 (9)
       57 |
     - 54 |  6 (9)
        3 | 36 (9)
```

But if you estimate first, it is much easier to use the shorter way.

2 Copy and complete these:

```
          □ r □
   a 8 ) 346
       -320 | □ (8)
         □  |
       - □  | □ (8)
         □  | □ (8)
```

```
          □
   b 7 ) 357
       - □  | 50 (7)
         □  |
       - □  | □ (7)
         □  | □ (7)
```

```
          □ r □
   c 9 ) 645
       -630 | □ (9)
         □  |
       - □  | □ (9)
         □  | □ (9)
```

d $517 \div 6$ **f** $434 \div 7$ **h** $435 \div 5$ **j** $647 \div 8$ **l** $554 \div 6$

e $223 \div 5$ **g** $516 \div 8$ **i** $522 \div 9$ **k** $826 \div 9$ **m** $365 \div 7$

l Now try these (remember to estimate first):

a In a forest 294 trees are planted in 7 rows.
How many are in each row?

b If £448 is shared equally among 8 boys
how much will each receive?

c There are 485 car tyres in a warehouse.
How many cars would they provide tyres for?
(Don't forget the spare wheel.)

d The perimeter of a regular octagon is 344cm.
How long is one side?

e How many 5 millilitre spoonfuls of medicine can be poured
from a bottle holding 285ml?

f A machine makes a toy every 8 minutes.
How many does it make in 2 hours?

g How many egg boxes, each holding 6 eggs, will be needed
to pack 504 eggs?

h A ribbon 9cm wide has an area of 162cm².
How long is it?

i How many pens costing 8p each can you buy for £1.84?

j How many marbles, each weighing 7 grams, will weigh 168 grams?

Chapter 8: Length 1

Remember:

There are 10dm in 1 metre so $1dm = \frac{1}{10}m = 0.1m$	There are 100cm in 1m so $1cm = \frac{1}{100}m = 0.01m$

The perimeter of this shape is 163cm. Add the lengths of the sides to check that this is correct.

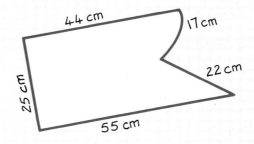

$$163cm = 100cm + 60cm + 3cm$$
$$= 1m + 6dm + 3cm$$
$$= 1m + \frac{6}{10}m + \frac{3}{100}m$$
$$= 1.00m + 0.60m + 0.03m$$
$$= 1.63m$$

The abacus picture shows 1·63 metres.

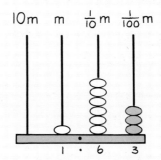

1 Find the perimeters of these shapes in metres.
Record your answers in the same way with an abacus picture.

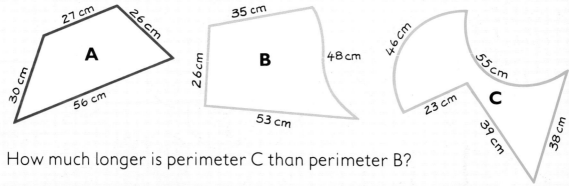

2 How much longer is perimeter C than perimeter B?

3 What is the difference between the perimeters of B and A?

4 The perimeter of a triangle is 1·25m. Two of the sides are 38cm and 45cm. Find the length of the third side.

Multiplication of metres and centimetres

An **equilateral** triangle has all its sides the same length.
To find the perimeter we can multiply the length of one side by 3.

Estimate first:

39cm ≃ 40cm,
so perimeter ≃ 120cm
      or 1·20m

Is the estimate ⟵
a good one?

```
        39
    ×    3
       27 (9cm × 3)
       90 (30cm × 3)
      117cm or 1·17m
```

39cm

39cm

39cm

39cm

I Use the same method of recording to find the perimeters of
equilateral triangles with sides of **a** 54cm, **b** 83cm, **c** 67cm.
Estimate each answer first.

2 A **polygon** is a flat shape with many corners and sides
('poly' means 'many' and 'gon' means 'corner').
Find some more words beginning with 'poly-' meaning 'many'.

3 A **regular** polygon has equal sides and equal angles.
Use multiplication to find the perimeters of these polygons in metres.
Remember to **estimate** first.

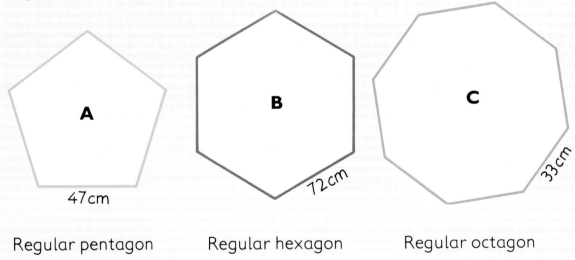

A   47cm   Regular pentagon

B   72cm   Regular hexagon

C   33cm   Regular octagon

4 What do 'penta', 'hexa' and 'octa' mean?

I These polygons have equal sides but they are not regular.

  a Why not?   **b** Are they symmetrical?

  c First estimate and then work out their perimeters in metres.

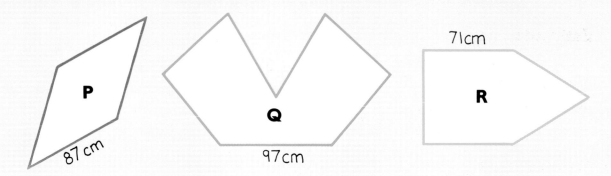

Sometimes measurements are given in metres and parts of a metre.
(Estimate 4+4+2+3 = 13m)

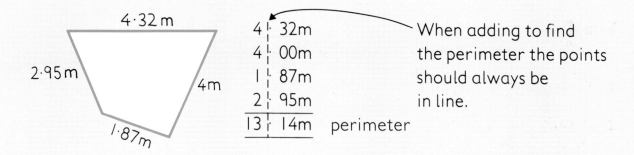

```
4 ¦ 32m
4 ¦ 00m
1 ¦ 87m
2 ¦ 95m
13 ¦ 14m   perimeter
```

When adding to find
the perimeter the points
should always be
in line.

2 Estimate and then find the perimeter of a pentagon whose sides are
3·25m, 4·03m, 2m, 3·87m and 2·60m.

This square has sides 4·78m long.
To find the perimeter multiply 4·78 by 4.
(Estimate: 4·78 ≃ 5m   5m × 4 = 20m)

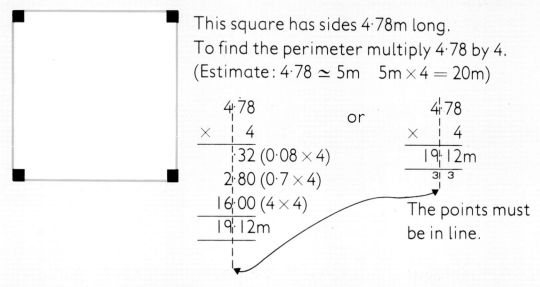

```
  4·78
×   4
  ·32 (0·08 × 4)
 2·80 (0·7 × 4)
16·00 (4 × 4)
19·12m
```

or

```
  4·78
×   4
 19·12m
 3¦ 3
```

The points must
be in line.

3 Estimate and then find the perimeter of a regular hexagon
whose sides are 2·14 metres long.

Division of metres and centimetres

The perimeter of this square is 1·28m.
The sides are equal in length so to find
the length of one side, we divide the perimeter by 4.

1·28m ÷ 4 = 128cm ÷ 4

(Estimate: 'just over 120' ÷ 4
is 'just over 30',
so length of side ≃ 30cm.)

Length of side = 32cm or 0·32m.

```
           32
   4 ) 128
      −120 | 30 (4)
         8
    −    8 |  2 (4)
        32
```

I Find the lengths of sides of squares with these perimeters.
Give each answer first in cm then in m.

  a 1·24m   **b** 2·88m   **c** 7·64m   **d** 4·04m   **e** 5·68m

2 For each of these regular polygons find the length of one side.
Give each answer first in cm then in m.

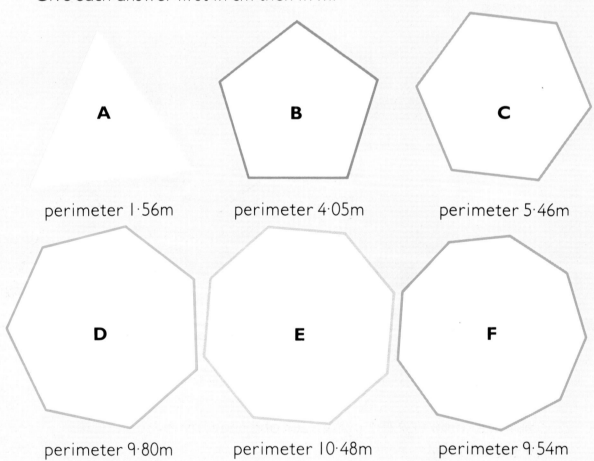

perimeter 1·56m   perimeter 4·05m   perimeter 5·46m

perimeter 9·80m   perimeter 10·48m   perimeter 9·54m

Jane cuts a rope, 13·80 metres long, into quarters
to make four skipping ropes of equal length.
How long is each skipping rope?

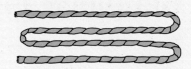

$\frac{1}{4}$ of 13·80 metres = 13·80 ÷ 4

(Estimate: 13·80m ≃ 14m; 14 ÷ 4 = $3\frac{1}{2}$.*)

First change 13·80m to cm then divide by 4.
Each skipping rope is 345cm or 3·45m long.

* (Was the estimate a good one?)

```
           345cm
      4 ) 1380cm
       -1200   300 (4)
          180
       -  160    40 (4)
           20
           20     5 (4)
                345 (4)
```

I How long would each be if Jane wanted to make 5 equal skipping ropes
  from 13·80 metres?

2 How long is $\frac{1}{6}$ of 13·80 metres?

3 Give the answers to these in metres:

  a 10·43m ÷ 7   **c** 477cm ÷ 3   **e** 28·98m ÷ 9
  b 16·02m ÷ 6   **d** 11m ÷ 4   **f** 13dm ÷ 5

4 A loop of string is pegged out to make a regular hexagon
  with sides 1·25m long.

  a How long is the string?

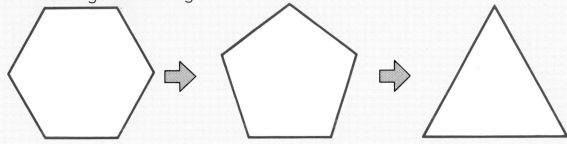

  b If the same loop is pegged out to make a regular pentagon,
    how long will one side be?
  c If an equilateral triangle is made from the same loop
    how long will its side be?
  d Compare the sides of the hexagon and the triangle.
    What do you notice?

Chapter 9: Money

1 Write the following amounts in pounds—the first is done for you.

a 435p = £4·35   **c** 574p   **e** 891p   **g** 73p
b 603p   **d** 306p   **f** 1024p   **h** 92p

2 Write the following amounts in pence:

a £1·73   **c** £6·37   **e** £9·37   **g** £0·61
b £3·49   **d** £8·94   **f** £10·61   **h** £0·17

Estimate first by rounding to the nearest £.

3 Copy and add these amounts

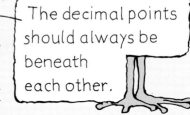

a £	**b** £	**c** £	**d** £
4·73	3·61	1·94	3·42
+2·69	+1·49	+6·87	+5·71
1·58	7·82	7·82	3·94

The decimal points should always be beneath each other.

e £3·72+£1·96+£5·83   **f** £4·91+£1·37+£6·73

4 Copy and subtract these amounts
—the points should always be beneath each other:

a £	**b** £	**c** £	**d** £	**e** £	**f** £
6·73	3·96	4·23	3·91	6·23	8·02
−4·22	−1·43	−2·17	−1·88	−4·37	−4·80

Multiplication of £ by single digit

£3·62×7

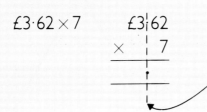

```
£3 62
×   7
─────
```

The points should always be beneath each other so first place the point in the answer line. Then multiply.

```
    £3·62
×       7
─────────
   £25·34
    ·4 1
```

5 Multiply these in the same way

a £1·32×3   **c** £3·51×5   **e** £4·78×8   **g** £2·19×8   **i** £5·87×9
b £1·74×2   **d** £0·76×6   **f** £3·54×7   **h** £3·44×6   **j** £4·96×7

k How much would you pay for five records if each one costs £3·59?

l If you were given a £10 gift voucher to spend at a record shop, would you be able to buy four cassettes each costing £2·49?

m What would it cost to rent a boat for seven days at £6·35 for a day?

Division by single digits

£8·96 ÷ 7
(Estimate: £9 ÷ 7 is just over £1)
We write the amount without
its decimal point and divide
as we have done before:

```
        128
    7 ) 896
      -700 | 100 (7)
       196
      -140 |  20 (7)
        56
      - 56 |   8 (7)
             128 (7)
```

After dividing put the decimal point back in to the amount we started with.

Following the rule that decimal points are in the same column put a point in the answer.
The answer is £1·28.

```
        1·28
    7 ) 8·96
      -700 | 100 (7)
       196
      -140 |  20 (7)
        56
      - 56 |   8 (7)
             128 (7)
```

1 Divide these the same way. Remember: estimate, calculate, check.
  a £5·25 ÷ 3   **d** £7·25 ÷ 3   **g** £9·14 ÷ 6   **j** £9·44 ÷ 8
  b £2·78 ÷ 2   **e** £4·12 ÷ 3   **h** £6·36 ÷ 7   **k** £11·32 ÷ 10
  c £6·36 ÷ 4   **f** £8·73 ÷ 5   **i** £10·12 ÷ 9   **l** £12·47 ÷ 8

  m Three copies of a book cost £7·35. How much does each one cost?

  n A boarding house charges £43·40 for a week's bed and breakfast. What is the cost per day?

  o How much does one shirt cost if I pay £20·85 for three?

  p If I am paid £14·70 for 6 hours work, how much an hour is this?

1 Find the total cost of these using the prices
on the catalogue pages:

a Rubber torch   **b** Fork   **c** Shears
    Sports bag   Spade   Watering can
    Table tennis set _____   Rake _____   Hose

                  _____   _____   _____

2 Which costs more and by how much?

   a Vacuum flask or shears
   b Table tennis set or sports bag
   c Badminton racquet or wheelbarrow
   d Lawn edger or rake

3 Find the cost of:

   a 4 spades   **c** 6 hoses   **e** 8 vacuum flasks
   b 3 sports bags   **d** 5 badminton racquets   **f** 7 shears

1 Copy and complete the following bills:

   a 4 spades
     3 forks
     5 lawn edgers _____
     Total _____

   b 5 table tennis sets
     7 badminton racquets
     4 sports bags
     Total _____

   c 8 torches
     6 hoses
     5 watering cans _____
     Total _____

   d 3 wheelbarrows
     6 shears
     5 rakes _____
     Total _____

2 If I buy 3 torches and a vacuum flask,
how much change should I get from a £10 note?

3 Here is a bill from last year.
What was the price last year for:

   a one torch.
   b one vacuum flask.
   c a sports bag.
   d one badminton racquet?

4 How much dearer is each item in
the bill this year?

5 Make out a similar bill using
this year's prices. How much
more is the total this year?

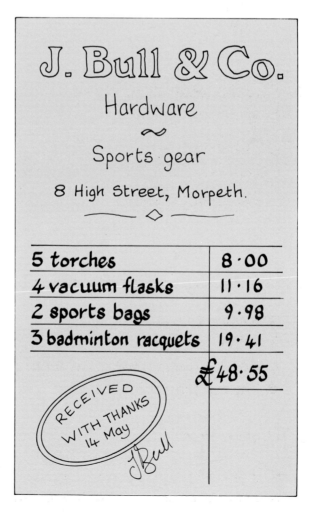

J. Bull & Co.

Hardware

~

Sports gear

8 High Street, Morpeth.

——— ◇ ———

5 torches	8·00
4 vacuum flasks	11·16
2 sports bags	9·98
3 badminton racquets	19·41
	£48·55

RECEIVED
WITH THANKS
14 May

Chapter 10: Rounding off

Rulers, tape-measures, clock faces, protractors, measuring jars,
dial scales etc. are all like a number line.
They have equally spaced marks to help us read off measurements.

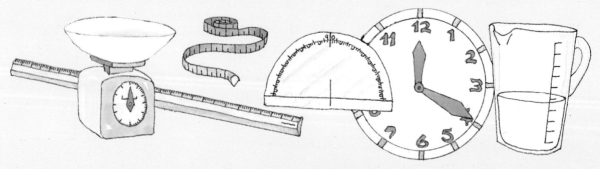

Sometimes a reading is between two marks.
To get an **approximate** answer we can **round up**
or **round down** to the nearest mark.

Approximate
means 'close to'
or 'nearly correct'.

Here is a part of a number line showing half-way
marks between the whole numbers.

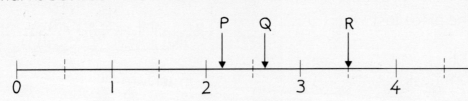

Because P is nearer to 2 than 3, it has an approximate reading of 2
to the nearest whole number (rounding down).

Q is nearer to 3 than 2; its approximate reading is 3
to the nearest whole number (rounding up).

R is on the half-way mark between 3 and 4. It is rounded up
to the approximate reading of 4.

I   Write the approximate reading, to the nearest whole number,
for these letters:

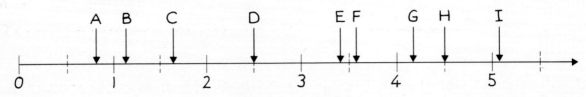

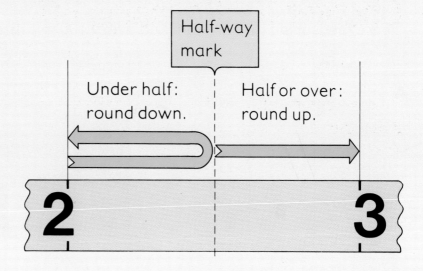

This diagram shows the rule for rounding up or rounding down.

Half-way mark

Under half: round down.

Half or over: round up.

Some rulers are marked in half centimetres or in centimetres (cm) and millimetres (mm). 10mm = 1cm, so the half-way mark is 5mm along.

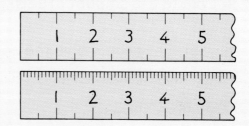

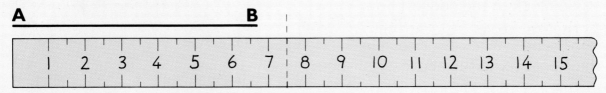

Line AB is 7cm *to the nearest centimetre*.
Line AB ≃ 7cm.   ≃ means "is approximately equal to".

1   Measure these lines to the nearest cm. Use the ≃ sign to record the lengths. The first one is done for you.

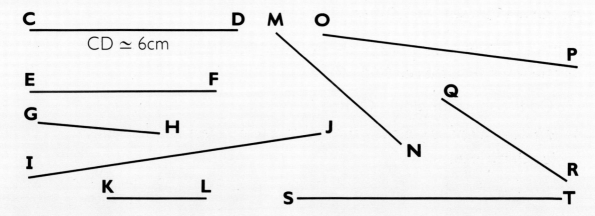

CD ≃ 6cm

2   Measure the length and breadth of this book to the nearest centimetre.

These measuring jars are marked every 100 millilitres (ml).

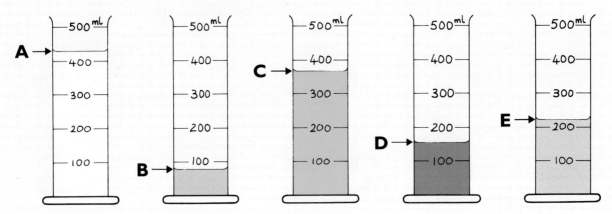

I Write the amount in each jar to the nearest 100ml. Use the ≃ sign.

Sometimes people give the approximate time shown on a clock. They often say, "It's just gone four o'clock" or "It's nearly ten past."

This clock shows:
six o'clock to the nearest hour.
   (nearer to six o'clock than 7);

half-past six to the nearest half-hour.
   (nearer to 6.30 than 6 o'clock);

quarter past six to the nearest quarter-hour.
   (nearer to $\frac{1}{4}$ past than $\frac{1}{2}$ past);

6.20 to the nearest 5 minutes.
   (nearer to 6.20 than 6.25).

2 Write the approximate time shown on clock, P

    a to the nearest hour.   **c** to the nearest $\frac{1}{4}$ hour.
    b to the nearest $\frac{1}{2}$ hour.   **d** to the nearest 5 minutes.

Do the same for clocks Q, R, S.

Rounding off decimal numbers

When rounding off decimal numbers to the nearest whole number,
0·5 is the half-way mark.

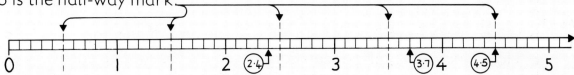

2·4 to the nearest whole number is 2·0 (rounding down).
3·7 to the nearest whole number is 4·0 (rounding up).
4·5 to the nearest whole number is 5·0 (rounding up).

I Write these to the nearest whole number:

a 2·7	**c** 26·9	**e** 7·5	**g** 9·6	**i** 7·06
b 4·1	**d** 0·8	**f** 3·25	**h** 99·9	**j** 4·005

Rounding off calculator answers

As we are rounding off to the nearest whole number, we must look at the
first figure after the decimal point. But 6.525 is just over 6.5, so 6.525 ≃ 7

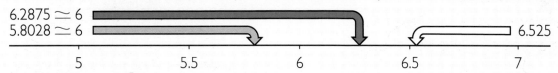

2 Write these calculator answers to the nearest whole number:

   a 2.825   **b** 8.499   **c** 124.666   **d** 17.5245   **e** 99.62   **f** 19.5025

3 **Without using a calculator**, write the answers to these:
   (No need to estimate; no need to calculate—take a short cut.)
   a $20 \div 5 \times 5$ **b** $7 \div 4 \times 4$ **c** $7 \div 3 \times 3$ **d** $24 \div 6 \times 6$ **e** $24 \div 7 \times 7$

4 Now repeat question **3** but this time use a calculator.
   Compare the results. What do you notice?

   $7 \div 4 = 1.75$ and $1.75 \times 4 = 7$

   but $7 \div 3 = 2.333333333$ on and on without end.
   But the calculator **does end** when all the spaces in the
   display are filled.
   The calculator works out $2.3333333 \times 3 = 6.9999999$,
   which we have to round up to 7.

5 Use the calculator for these. Record the answer then round it to the
   nearest whole number.
   a $9 \div 3 \times 3$ **b** $9 \div 7 \times 7$ **c** $5 \div 9 \times 9$ **d** $81 \div 11 \times 11$
   e $60 \div 13 \times 13$ **f** $54 \div 17 \times 17$ **g** $1 \div 6 \times 6$ **h** $2 \div 6 \times 6$
   i $3 \div 6 \times 6$ **j** $4 \div 6 \times 6$ **k** $5 \div 6 \times 6$

   Explain what is different about questions **a** and **i** and why.

1 First estimate the answer to the nearest £ then work out the exact answer and compare it with your estimate.
  a The cost of 3 pairs of socks at £1.99 a pair.
  b If 4 bags of sweets cost £7.60, what is the cost of one bag?
  c How much will half a dozen handkerchiefs cost at 85p each?
  d Four people each hired a bicycle for two hours.
     The total charge was £10. How much an hour is this?

2 Here is a print-out from a supermarket.
First round each item to the nearest £. Then make an estimate of the total by adding the estimates.
How close is your estimate to the real total?

6 EGGS	0.65
CORNFLAKES	1.35
BEEF JOINT	6.28
2 TINS PEARS @ 1.55	3.10
KITCHENWARE	2.99
TOILET TISSUES	1.50
TOTAL	————

3 If lengths in m and cm are rounded off to the nearest metre, what is the half-way mark?

4 Write these lengths to the nearest metre:
  a 3m 15cm   **c** six and a half metres   **e** 375cm   **g** 13·26m
  b 7m 82cm   **d** 6·05 metres   **f** 68cm   **h** 29·85m

5 **a** Find the perimeter of this isosceles triangle.
   b Round off the perimeter to the nearest metre.
   c This time round off the length of each side to the nearest metre. Then add these rounded off lengths to find the perimeter in metres.
   d Compare your answers to **b** and **c**.
  Write a sentence about your results.

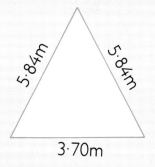

5·84m   5·84m

3·70m

6 Make some measurements in your classroom and record them in a table like this:

distance	m	cm	approx. length to nearest metre
length of classroom breadth height of door			

Approximate area

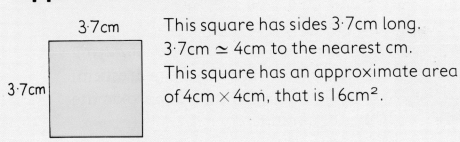

3·7cm

3·7cm

This square has sides 3·7cm long.
3·7cm ≃ 4cm to the nearest cm.
This square has an approximate area
of 4cm × 4cm, that is 16cm².

1 Calculate the approximate area of
these figures (not drawn to scale).
You must first round up or
round down as necessary.
Remember:
for less than ·5, round **down**
for ·5 or more, round **up**.

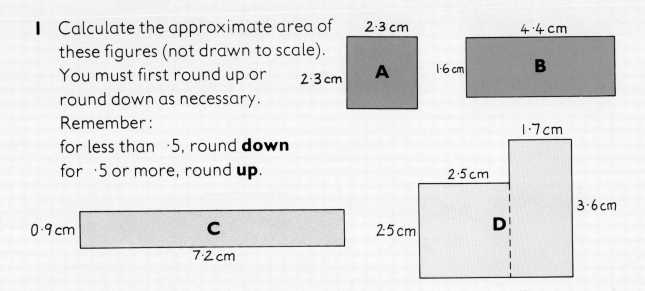

2 A piece of ribbon 2cm wide has an approximate area of 16cm² to
the nearest cm².
What is the shortest length it can have?

3 A small bedroom measures 3·8m wide and 5·2m long.
  a Would 15m² of carpet be sufficient to cover the floor?
  b What would be the least area of carpet, to the nearest m²,
    that you would need to buy?
  c Calculate the cost of the carpet at £9·50 per m².

4 Find the approximate areas (to the nearest square metre) of the floors
of rectangular rooms, corridors, etc. Record in a table like this:

	length m	cm	length to nearest m	breadth m	cm	breadth to nearest m	approx. area in m²
my bedroom	4	80	5 m	3	25	3 m	15 m²
classroom							

Approximate volume

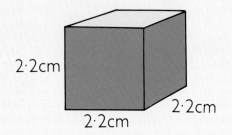

This cube has edges of 2·2cm.
2·2 ≃ 2cm (to the nearest cm).
The cube has an approximate volume
of 2cm × 2cm × 2cm, that is 8cm³.

1 Find the approximate volume of cubes with edges of:

a 1·9cm **b** 3·3cm **c** 9·6cm **d** 5·9cm **e** 4·5cm

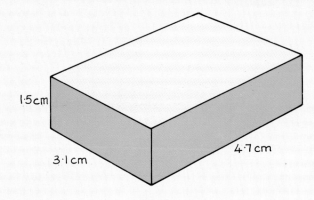

To find the approximate volume of this cuboid, first round off
each measurement to nearest cm:

5cm × 3cm × 2cm

The approximate volume is 30cm³.

2 Find the approximate volume of each cuboid:

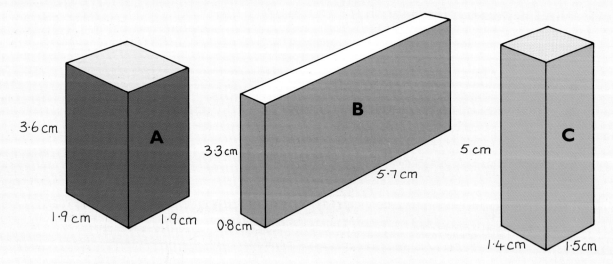

3 Measure the length, breadth and height of your classroom to
the nearest metre. Find the approximate volume in m³.

Chapter 11: Area 2

Area of a triangle

1 On card carefully draw a rectangle 6cm long and 3cm wide.

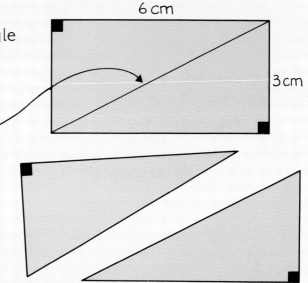

a Write down the area of the rectangle.
Draw a diagonal like this:
Carefully cut out the rectangle.
Now cut along the diagonal to make two right-angled triangles.
A right-angle is marked like this:

Check, without measuring, that the two triangles are the same size.

b Write down the area of each triangle.

c Copy and complete: The area of each triangle is [   ] the area of the rectangle.

2 Find the area of each of these triangles:

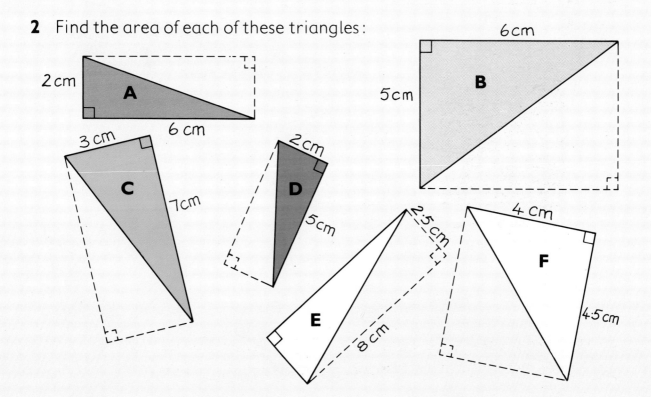

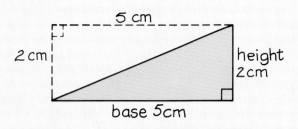

One side of this triangle, the **base**, is 5cm long.

The **height** of the triangle is always measured at right-angles to the **base**. It is the **perpendicular height**.

Area of **rectangle** is base × height
5cm × 2cm = 10cm²
Area of **triangle** is half the area of the rectangle
that is (base × height) ÷ 2
So the area of the **triangle** is 10cm² ÷ 2 = 5cm²

The area of a triangle is (base × height) ÷ 2

1 Find the areas of these right-angled triangles.
   Set them out like the example:

$$\text{Area of triangle A} = (b \times h) \div 2$$
$$= (4 \times 3) \div 2$$
$$= 12 \quad \div 2$$
$$= 6\text{cm}^2$$

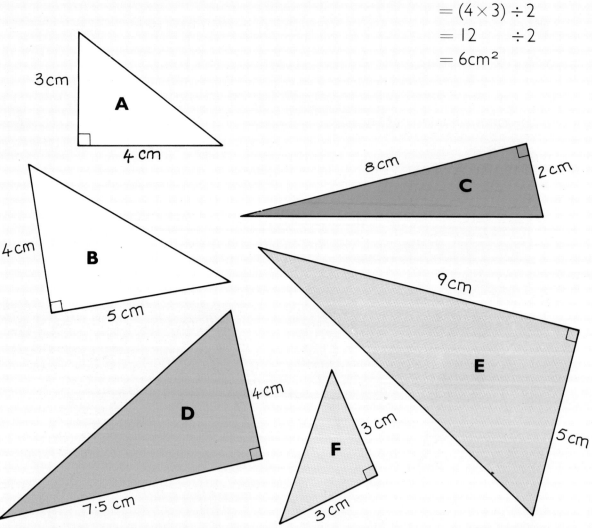

If a triangle is **not** right-angled, the height is still measured at **right-angles** to the base.

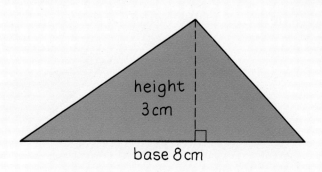

In this triangle:
the base is 8cm and
the perpendicular height is 3cm.

base 8cm

On cm-squared paper draw the triangle inside a rectangle like this:

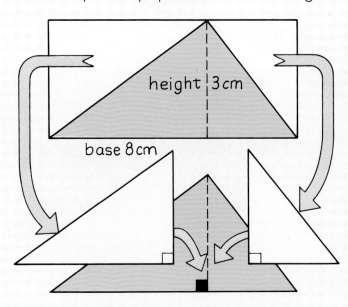

Cut out the rectangle. Then carefully cut off the two shaded triangles and turn them so that they fit together to cover the whole triangle.

The area of the brown triangle is **half** the area of the rectangle.
That is $(b \times h) \div 2$
$(8 \times 3) \div 2 = 24 \div 2 = 12$
Area of triangle is 12cm²

I On squared paper draw these rectangles and triangles.
Work out the area of each triangle.

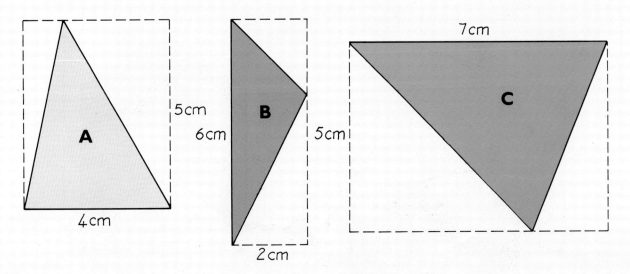

I Find the areas of these triangles. When the base or perpendicular height is not marked, measure it.

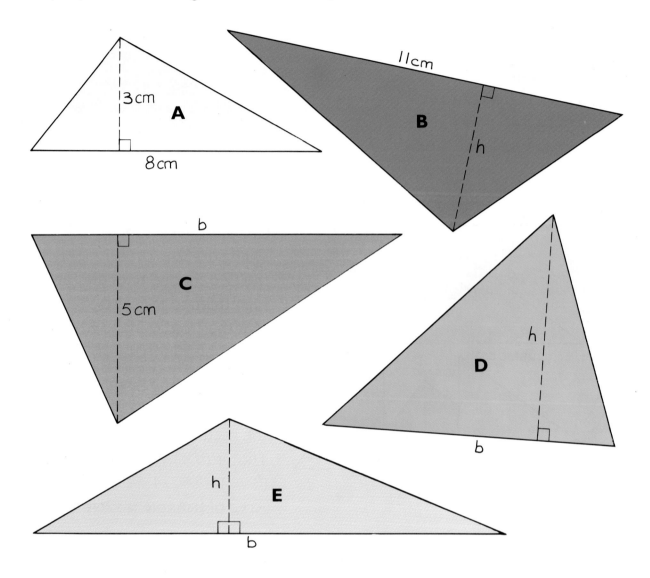

2 What is the area, in square metres, of the end wall of this house?

3 Find the area of this flower bed in m²

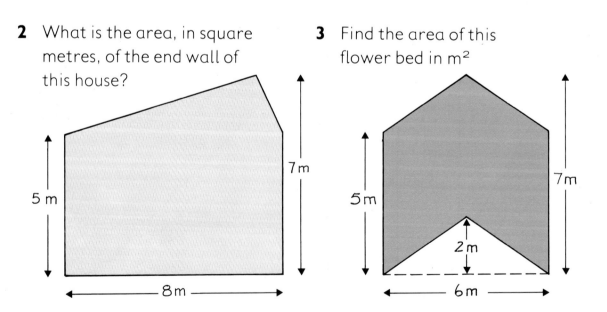

Chapter 12: Co-ordinates

Plotting points

I Copy this lattice on to centimetre squared paper using one square on your paper for one square in the diagram.

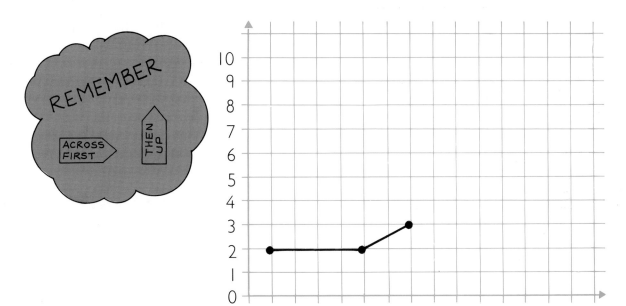

Mark and plot these points, joining them together as you plot them (the first three are drawn for you):

(1,2); (5,2); (7,3); (9,3); (10,4); (12,4); (14,5); (12,6); (10,6); (9,7); (7,7); (5,8); (1,8); (4,7); (4,3); (1,2).

2 Make another lattice on squared paper like the last one.
Mark and plot these points joining them together as you plot them.

(2,1); (2,6); (4,8); (6,8); (8,7); (10,8); (11,7); (12,4); (11,2); (10,2); (11,4); (10,5); (9,4); (9,1); (8,1); (8,4); (6,3); (3,4); (3,1); (2,1).

Then join (2,6) to (1,5),
and join (9,5) to (7,5) to (9,7).
Put an eye at (10,6).

3 Make up a picture of your own. List the points in order and give it to your friend for him to draw.

A straight line graph

$3 + 7 = 10$

$8 + 2 = 10$

These are two pairs of whole
numbers which add up to 10.
They can be written as:

(3,7); (8,2)

1 a Make a list of all the pairs
of numbers which add up to 10
—don't forget (0,10).

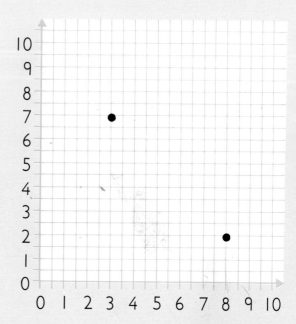

b Copy this lattice onto
centimetre squared paper
using a square centimetre
for each square in the diagram.
Notice that each number takes
two squares

c Plot the pairs of numbers you listed.
Two are done for you.

d The points you have marked should all lie on a straight line.
Draw the line.
The line is the graph of pairs of numbers which add up to ten.

e As two squares were used for one whole
number when we marked our lattice,
the squares between are used
for halves. Write them on your lattice
as in this diagram.

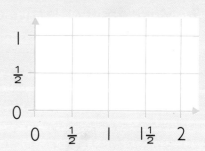

f Use the graph to complete these pairs of numbers which add up to 10:

$(7\frac{1}{2}, \square)$; $(\square, 3\frac{1}{2})$; $(1\frac{1}{2}, \square)$; $(5\frac{1}{2}, \square)$; $(\square, 9\frac{1}{2})$;

$(8\frac{1}{2}, \square)$; $(\square, 4\frac{1}{2})$.

Plotting shapes

1 **a** Copy the lattice in the diagram on to centimetre squared paper.

   b Mark and join together, in order, the points:
   (1,1); (5,1); (3,7); (1,1)

The shape drawn should be the isosceles triangle marked **a** on the diagram.

This shape has one axis of symmetry and it has been drawn on the figure with a dashed line.

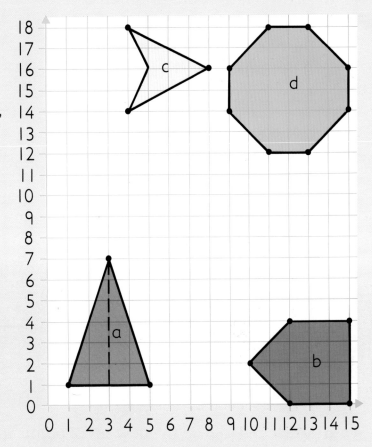

2 Copy the other three shapes onto the lattice making a list of the points plotted for each figure.
   With a dashed line, mark in any axes of symmetry.

3 Plot these points joining them together in order.
   Name the shape drawn and mark in any axes of symmetry.

   a (1,13); (4,13); (4,10); (1,10); (1,13).

   b (6,0); (9,0); (9,4); (6,4); (6,0).

   c (12,7); (12,11); (15,10); (15,6); (12,7).

   d (5,12); (6,14); (8,14); (9,12); (8,10); (6,10); (5,12).

   e (5,6); (11,6); (9,9); (5,9); (5,6).

Translations

1 a Draw a lattice on centimetre squared paper. Number the horizontal ⟶ axis from 0 to 10 and the vertical ↑ axis from 0–10.

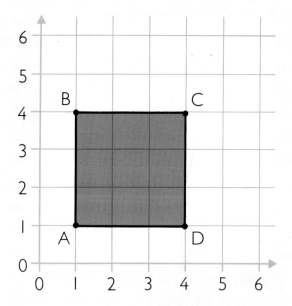

b Plot and join the points in order:
A (1,1); B (1,4); C (4,4); D (4,1); A (1,1).

c What shape have you drawn?

d What is the area of the shape?

2 Adding 4 to the first number in each pair gives us a new set of points:

Original set: A (1,1); B (1,4); C (4,4); D (4,1); A (1,1).

New set: A (5,1); B (5,4); C (8,4); D (8,1); A (5,1).

a Mark and join up the new set of points in a different colour.
b What shape have you drawn?
c What is its area?
d What has happened to the original shape?

3 a Make a new set of points by adding 5 to the second number in each pair of the **original** set.
b Mark and join up the new set of points in a different colour.
c What shape have you drawn?
d What is its area?
e What has happened to it?

4 a Make a new set of points by adding 4 to the first number and by adding 5 to the second number in each pair of the **original** set.
b Mark and join up the new set of points in a different colour.
c What shape have you drawn?
d What is its area?
e What has happened to it?

Enlargements

1 **a** Draw a lattice on centimetre-squared paper. Number the horizontal and vertical axes from 0 to 16.

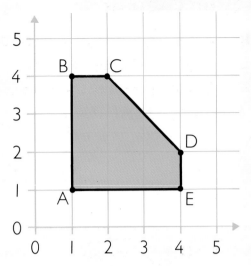

b Plot and join the points:
A (1,1); B (1,4); C (2,4);
D (4,2); E (4,1); A (1,1).

c What is the area of the shape?

2 Multiplying both numbers in each pair by 3 gives a new set of points:

Original set: A (1,1); B (1,4); C (2,4); D (4,2); E (4,1); A (1,1).

New set: A (3,3); B (3,12); C (6, 12); D (12, 6); E (12, 3); A (3,3).

a Mark, letter and join up with a different coloured crayon the new set of points.

b What is the area of the new shape?

c Multiplying the numbers by 3, multiplies the area by ▢

d Use a dashed line to join the two A's.

e Do the same for each of the other letters.

f Continue the dashed lines to the left. What happens?

3 **a** Multiply the original pairs by 2.

b Mark, letter and join up with another coloured crayon the new set of points.

c What do you notice about the new points?

d What is the area of the new shape?

e Multiplying the numbers by 2, multiplies the area by ▢

4 **a** Multiply the original set by 4, plot and join up the points.

b Multiplying the numbers by 4, multiplies the area by ▢

c Continue the dashed lines to the right. What happens?

Reflections

1 **a** Copy this lattice on to centimetre squared paper.

   b Plot these points:
   (4,4); (9,9); (1,1).

   c These points are on a straight line.
   Draw as much of the line as you can.

   d Using whole numbers only make a list of other points which are on the line.

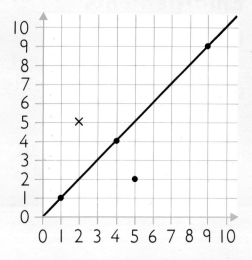

The point (5,2) has been marked on the lattice. If the line drawn is a mirror line or an axis of symmetry, there will be a reflection or matching point on the other side of the line. It is marked with a cross at (2,5).

2 Plot these points with dots and mark their reflections with crosses:

   a (8,4)   **d** (9,2)   **g** (7,8)
   b (3,7)   **e** (1,6)   **h** (9,5)
   c (5,3)   **f** (0,4)   **i** (2,7)

3 **a** Copy the lattice above on to centimetre squared paper.

   b Draw in the reflection line.

   c Plot and join in order these points:
   A (3,1); B (7,2); C (5,2); D (6,4); A (3,1)

   d Draw the reflection of this shape.

   e Copy and complete:

   Original points: A (3,1); B (7,2); C (5,2); D (6,4); A (3,1).

   New points: A (,); B (,); C (,); D (,); A (,).

4 What do you notice about these reflections?

Chapter 13: Weight

Nett weight and gross weight

This tin of peas weighs 520g but the label says 425g.
This means that the peas inside the tin
weigh 425g—this is the nett weight.
The peas and the tin together weigh 520g—
this is called the gross weight.

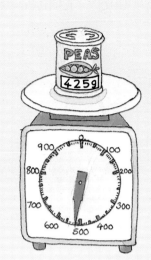

1 How much will the empty tin weigh?

2 a Copy and complete this table
for other tins of food.

b What is the total gross weight
of all five full tins?
(Answer first in g then in kg.)

c What is the weight of
the heaviest empty tin?

	Gross weight	Nett weight	Weight of tin
peaches	1025g	822g	
carrots	520g	425g	
soup	490g		55g
beans		576g	158g
salmon	260g		47g

3 a How many grams does each small marking on the dial stand for?

b The pointers show the gross weight
of some more goods.

Make another table like
the one in question 2.

Nett weights are shown
in brackets.

A Chocolates (120g).
B Jelly (180g).
C Crunchies (375g).
D Cornflakes (500g).
E Jam (454g).
F Pears (792g).

c What is the weight of the lightest container?

1000g = 1 kilogram.

'kilo' comes from a Greek word meaning 'a thousand'.

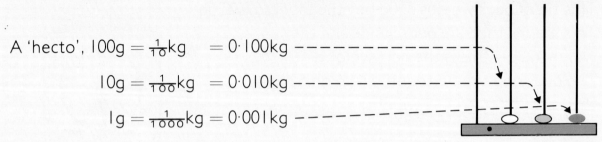

A 'hecto', 100g = $\frac{1}{10}$kg   = 0·100kg ------------

10g = $\frac{1}{100}$kg = 0·010kg ------------

1g = $\frac{1}{1000}$kg = 0·001kg ------------

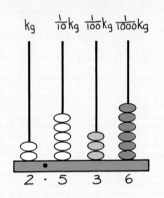

2536g = 2000g + 500g + 30g + 6g

     = 2kg + 0·500kg + 0·030kg + 0·006kg

     = 2·536kg

1 Draw abacus pictures of these weights and record them in kilograms:

  a 1234g   **c** 606g   **e** 4 hectos   **g** 15g
  b 325g   **d** 3030g   **f** half a kg   **h** 8g

2 Rewrite each of these lists so that the weights are in order with the heaviest at the top and the lightest at the bottom.
(Use the information at the top of this page to help you.)

a 30g	**b** 0·200kg	**c** 27g	**d** half a kg
$\frac{9}{10}$kg	$\frac{7}{100}$kg	$\frac{4}{100}$kg	$\frac{75}{100}$kg
0·060kg	19g	0·300kg	720g
50g	0·090kg	$\frac{2}{1000}$kg	7 'hectos'
4 'hectos'	60g	80g	0·725kg

3 Find the total of the weights in each list.

1

This cake weighs 2·270kg.

In an 'estimate the weight of the cake' competition, these weights were recorded:

A 2kg	E 2·500kg
B 1½kg	F 1700g
C 227g	G 22·700kg
D 1kg 900g	H 2kg 27g

a Which estimate is the 'winner'?

b Which is the second nearest?

c Write the estimates in order starting with the heaviest.

d How much heavier is the largest estimate than the smallest?

When rounding off weights to the nearest kilogram:

for 0·500kg and over, round **up**.
for less than 0·500kg, round **down**.

For example: 2·360kg ≃ 2kg; 3·635 ≃ 4kg

2 Write these weights to the nearest kg:

   a 2·426kg   **b** 1·830kg   **c** 4·050kg   **d** 0·680kg   **e** 1245g

3 Rounding off to the nearest kilogram helps to work out the approximate total weight of several parcels.

   a Add the rounded off weights of these five parcels to find the **approximate** total weight.

   b Find the **actual** total weight.

   c What is the difference between the two totals?

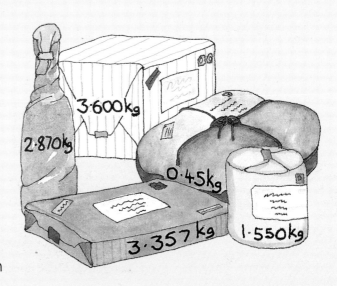

Multiplication of kg and g

The gross weight of
a tin of plums is 1·135kg.
To find the total weight
of 5 tins, multiply
1·135kg by 5.
(Estimate: 1·135kg × 5
≃ 5·500kg)

$$
\begin{array}{r}
1{\cdot}135\text{kg} \\
\times\quad 5 \\
\hline
{\cdot}025 \\
{\cdot}150 \\
{\cdot}500 \\
5{\cdot}000 \\
\hline
5{\cdot}675\text{kg}
\end{array}
\qquad
\begin{array}{l}
({\cdot}005 \times 5) \\
({\cdot}030 \times 5) \\
({\cdot}100 \times 5) \\
(1{\cdot}000 \times 5)
\end{array}
$$

or

$$
\begin{array}{r}
1{\cdot}135\text{kg} \\
\times\quad 5 \\
\hline
5{\cdot}675\text{kg} \\
{}_{1\ 2}
\end{array}
$$

The decimal
points
must be in line.

1   The nett weight of the plums in each tin is 937 grams.
    What is the total nett weight of the plums from 5 tins?

2   Find the difference between the total gross weight and the total nett
    weight of 7 tins of pears if 1 tin has a gross weight of 1·025 and a nett
    weight of 792g. (Estimate first.)

Division of kg and g

If 4 bottles of lemonade weigh 2·328kg what does 1 bottle weigh?
(Estimate: 2·400 ÷ 4 = 0·600, so 2·328kg ÷ 4 is just under 0·600)

Working in kilograms:

$$
\begin{array}{r}
0{\cdot}582\text{kg} \\
4\,\overline{)\ 2{\cdot}328\text{kg}} \\
-2{\cdot}000 \\
\hline
0{\cdot}328 \\
-0{\cdot}320 \\
\hline
0{\cdot}008 \\
-0{\cdot}008 \\
\hline
\end{array}
\begin{array}{l}
\\
\\
0{\cdot}500 \times 4 \\
\\
0{\cdot}080 \times 4 \\
\\
0{\cdot}002 \times 4 \\
\hline
0{\cdot}582\text{kg}
\end{array}
$$

or

Working in grams:

$$
\begin{array}{r}
582\text{g} = 0{\cdot}582\text{kg} \\
4\,\overline{)\ 2328\text{g}} \\
-2000 \\
\hline
328 \\
-\ 320 \\
\hline
8 \\
-\ \ 8 \\
\hline
\end{array}
\begin{array}{l}
\\
\\
500 \times 4 \\
\\
80 \times 4 \\
\\
2 \times 4 \\
\hline
582\text{g}
\end{array}
$$

3   Find the weight of 1 packet of soap-powder if the total weight of 6
    packets is 13·860kg.

4   5 tins of tomatoes weigh 3·695kg and 7 tins of beans weigh 5·075kg.
    Which is heavier, a tin of tomatoes or a tin of beans, and by how much?

Chapter 14: Fractions 1

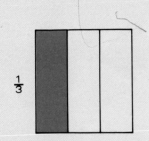 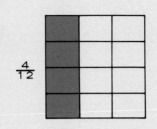 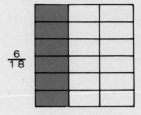

These diagrams show $\frac{1}{3}$, $\frac{4}{12}$ and $\frac{6}{18}$.
They are all members of the same family—the family of $\frac{1}{3}$.

1 a Draw diagrams to show $\frac{2}{6}, \frac{3}{9}, \frac{5}{15}$.
  b Do these three fractions belong to the family of $\frac{1}{3}$?

2 Copy and complete:
  a $7 \times 1 = \square$ **c** $1010 \times 1 = \square$ **e** $\frac{1}{5} \times 1 = \square$
  b $10 \times 1 = \square$ **d** $\frac{1}{2} \times 1 = \square$ **f** $\frac{1}{10} \times 1 = \square$

Multiplying a number by one leaves its value unchanged.

3 a $7 \div 1 = \square$ **c** $1010 \div 1 = \square$ **e** $\frac{1}{5} \div 1 = \square$
   b $10 \div 1 = \square$ **d** $\frac{1}{2} \div 1 = \square$ **f** $\frac{1}{10} \div 1 = \square$

Dividing a number by one leaves its value unchanged.

'The family of one'

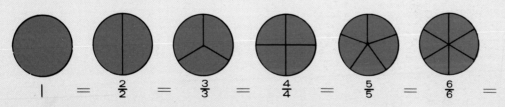

$$1 \quad = \quad \frac{2}{2} \quad = \quad \frac{3}{3} \quad = \quad \frac{4}{4} \quad = \quad \frac{5}{5} \quad = \quad \frac{6}{6} \quad =$$

$$\frac{1}{2} \times \left(\frac{3}{3}\right) = \frac{1 \times 3}{2 \times 3} = \frac{3}{6}, \text{ so } \frac{1}{2} = \frac{3}{6}$$

$$\frac{1}{4} \times \left(\frac{5}{5}\right) = \frac{1 \times 5}{4 \times 5} = \frac{5}{20}, \text{ so } \frac{1}{4} = \frac{5}{20}$$

$$\frac{20}{30} = \frac{2 \times 10}{3 \times 10} = \frac{2}{3} \times \left(\frac{10}{10}\right) = \frac{2}{3}, \text{ so } \frac{20}{30} = \frac{2}{3}$$

$$\frac{18}{24} = \frac{3 \times 6}{4 \times 6} = \frac{3}{4} \times \left(\frac{6}{6}\right) = \frac{3}{4}, \text{ so } \frac{18}{24} = \frac{3}{4}$$

The value of a fraction is unchanged
if we multiply or divide
the numerator (number above the line)
and the denominator (number below
the line) by the same number.

Numerator $\longrightarrow$ $\dfrac{3}{4} = \dfrac{\square}{24}$

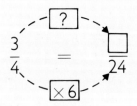

Denominator $\longrightarrow$

For these to be equal,
the numerator must be multiplied by 6
because the denominator has been multiplied by 6.

$$\frac{3}{4} = \frac{3 \times 6}{4 \times 6} = \frac{\boxed{18}}{24}$$

$$\frac{15}{20} = \frac{3}{\square}$$

The numerator has been divided by 5,
so the denominator must be divided by 5.

$$\frac{15}{20} = \frac{(15 \div 5)}{(20 \div 5)} = \frac{3}{\boxed{4}}$$

1 Copy and complete:

a $\dfrac{3}{4} = \dfrac{\square}{8}$

b $\dfrac{8}{12} = \dfrac{2}{\square}$

c $\dfrac{4}{5} = \dfrac{16}{\square}$

d $\dfrac{21}{28} = \dfrac{\square}{4}$

e $\dfrac{2}{3} = \dfrac{18}{\square}$

f $\dfrac{70}{100} = \dfrac{\square}{10}$

g $\dfrac{3}{5} = \dfrac{9}{\square}$

h $\dfrac{12}{16} = \dfrac{3}{\square}$

i $\dfrac{3}{10} = \dfrac{9}{\square}$

j $\dfrac{22}{33} = \dfrac{2}{\square}$

k $\dfrac{2}{5} = \dfrac{\square}{35}$

l $\dfrac{12}{28} = \dfrac{\square}{7}$

m $\dfrac{1}{2} = \dfrac{\square}{32}$

n $\dfrac{36}{42} = \dfrac{6}{\square}$

o $\dfrac{5}{8} = \dfrac{\square}{24}$

p $\dfrac{32}{40} = \dfrac{4}{\square}$

q $\dfrac{5}{8} = \dfrac{30}{\square}$

r $\dfrac{35}{50} = \dfrac{\square}{10}$

s $\dfrac{7}{8} = \dfrac{\square}{56}$

t $\dfrac{27}{45} = \dfrac{\square}{5}$

1 For each diagram write down the fraction shaded and the name of the family to which the fraction belongs:

Example: Fraction shaded $\frac{2}{6}$
Fraction family $\frac{1}{3}$

a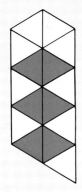

b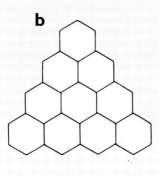

c

d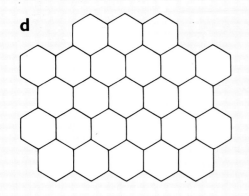

e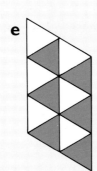

f

Addition

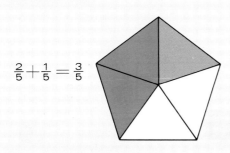

$\frac{2}{5}+\frac{1}{5}=\frac{3}{5}$

This is easy because we are thinking of 'fifths' and adding 'two fifths' to 'one fifth' to make 'three fifths'.

2 Copy and complete:

a $\frac{4}{7}+\frac{2}{7}=\boxed{}$

b $\frac{3}{8}+\frac{4}{8}=\boxed{}$

c $\frac{\boxed{}}{6}+\frac{5}{6}=1$

d $\frac{2}{9}+\frac{4}{9}+\frac{1}{9}=\boxed{}$

e $\frac{2}{11}+\frac{\boxed{}}{11}=\frac{9}{11}$

f $\frac{4}{13}+\frac{1}{13}+\frac{\boxed{}}{13}=\frac{8}{13}$

Subtraction

This is also easy when we are comparing the same kind of things.

e.g. $\frac{4}{7} - \frac{1}{7} = \frac{3}{7}$ We compare 'one-seventh' with 'four-sevenths'—it is 'three-sevenths' less.

1 Copy and complete:

a $\frac{5}{8} - \frac{3}{8} = \square$

d $\frac{4}{7} - \frac{2}{7} = \square$

g $\frac{7}{9} - \frac{2}{9} = \square$

b $\frac{\square}{6} - \frac{1}{6} = \frac{4}{6}$

e $\frac{7}{11} - \frac{2}{11} - \frac{1}{11} = \square$

h $\frac{11}{12} - \frac{10}{12} = \square$

c $\frac{7}{12} - \frac{5}{12} = \frac{\square}{12}$

f $\frac{7}{10} - \frac{3}{10} = \frac{\square}{10}$

i $\square - \frac{2}{9} = \frac{4}{9}$

2 **a** $\frac{7}{9} - \frac{2}{9} + \frac{4}{9} = \frac{\square}{9} = \square$

c $\frac{5}{12} + \frac{6}{12} - \frac{8}{12} = \frac{\square}{12} = \frac{1}{\square}$

b $\frac{17}{20} - \frac{11}{20} = \frac{\square}{20} = \frac{3}{\square}$

d $\frac{5}{8} - \frac{1}{8} = \frac{\square}{8} = \frac{1}{\square}$

Different denominators

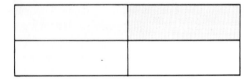

The diagram shows $\frac{1}{2} + \frac{1}{4} = \frac{3}{4}$

It is set down as: $\frac{1}{2} + \frac{1}{4} = \frac{2}{4} + \frac{1}{4}$

$= \frac{3}{4}$

This diagram shows $\frac{4}{5} - \frac{3}{10}$

It is set down as: $\frac{4}{5} - \frac{3}{10} = \frac{8}{10} - \frac{3}{10}$

$= \frac{5}{10}$

$= \frac{1}{2}$

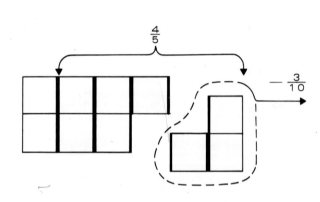

3 Do these in the same way:

a $\frac{1}{6} + \frac{5}{12}$ **c** $\frac{2}{3} - \frac{1}{12}$ **e** $\frac{7}{8} - \frac{11}{16}$ **g** $\frac{9}{10} - \frac{2}{5}$ **i** $\frac{2}{3} + \frac{1}{6}$

b $\frac{1}{2} + \frac{5}{16}$ **d** $\frac{4}{5} - \frac{7}{10}$ **f** $\frac{2}{3} + \frac{2}{15}$ **h** $\frac{3}{8} + \frac{5}{16}$ **j** $\frac{3}{4} - \frac{1}{16}$

$\frac{1}{2} + \frac{1}{3}$ is more difficult.

To find the common denominator we must look at the families of $\frac{1}{2}$ and $\frac{1}{3}$.

The family of $\frac{1}{2} = \{ \frac{1}{2}, \frac{2}{4}, \frac{3}{6}, \frac{4}{8}, \frac{5}{10}, \cdots \}$

The family of $\frac{1}{3} = \{ \frac{1}{3}, \frac{2}{6}, \frac{3}{9}, \frac{4}{12}, \frac{5}{15}, \cdots \}$

Looking along the lines we see that sixths are in both families.

$$\frac{1}{2} + \frac{1}{3} = \frac{3}{6} + \frac{2}{6}$$
$$= \frac{5}{6}$$

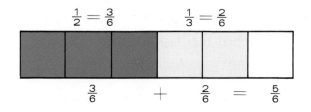

The family of $\frac{3}{5} = \{ \frac{3}{5}, \frac{6}{10}, \frac{9}{15}, \frac{12}{20}, \cdots \}$

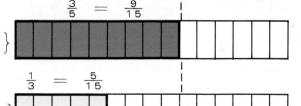

The family of $\frac{1}{3} = \{ \frac{1}{3}, \frac{2}{6}, \frac{3}{9}, \frac{4}{12}, \frac{5}{15}, \cdots \}$

$$\frac{3}{5} - \frac{1}{3}$$
$$= \frac{9}{15} - \frac{5}{15}$$
$$= \frac{4}{15}$$

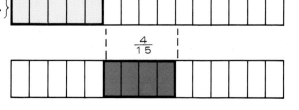

I Do these the same way.

a $\frac{1}{2} + \frac{1}{5}$ **d** $\frac{3}{4} - \frac{2}{3}$ **g** $\frac{3}{10} + \frac{2}{3}$ **j** $\frac{8}{9} - \frac{3}{4}$

b $\frac{1}{4} - \frac{1}{6}$ **e** $\frac{3}{8} + \frac{1}{3}$ **h** $\frac{7}{8} - \frac{2}{3}$ **k** $\frac{2}{5} + \frac{1}{4}$

c $\frac{2}{3} + \frac{1}{5}$ **f** $\frac{9}{10} - \frac{3}{4}$ **i** $\frac{2}{5} + \frac{1}{6}$ **l** $\frac{3}{4} - \frac{3}{5}$

Chapter 15 : Graphs

1   This graph shows how many people
attended the school play each night.
The hall will hold 100 people.
Tickets were 30p for adults
and 20p for children.

    a How many more were at the play
on Friday than on Tuesday?

    b Which was the most popular night?

    c Which was the least popular night?

    d What was the total attendance
for the five nights?

    e What fraction of the hall was
full on Tuesday night?

    f What fraction of the hall was
empty on Monday night?

    g If 32 children were at the play
on Friday what was the total
amount of money taken on Friday?

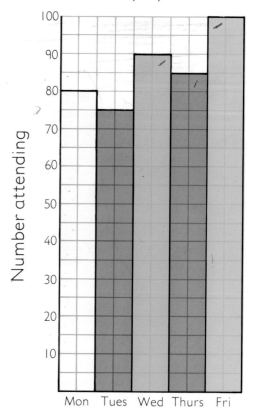

Graph showing attendance at school play.

2 **a** This table shows attendances each night. Copy and complete it.

Attendances	Monday	Tuesday	Wednesday	Thursday	Friday
Adults			59	58	
Children	30	28			32

    b What were the total receipts for the week?

3   Use these figures to draw a graph like the one above.

Attendances out of 32 for class 4	Monday		Tuesday		Wednesday		Thursday		Friday	
	a.m.	p.m.	a.m.	p.m.	a.m.	p.m.	a.m.	p.m.	a.m.	p.m.
	26	27	27	27	29	30	31	29	32	32

When you have drawn it make up some problems like those in question 1.

Pet	Tally	Total
Dogs	ⅢⅢ ⅢⅢ ⅢⅢ ⅢⅢ ⅢⅢ ⅢⅢ ⅢⅢ ⅢⅢ IIII	
Cats	ⅢⅢ ⅢⅢ ⅢⅢ ⅢⅢ III ⅢⅢ ⅢⅢ ⅢⅢ ⅢⅢ	
Budgerigars	ⅢⅢ III	
Tortoises	III	
Rabbits	ⅢⅢ II ⅢⅢ	
Hamsters	ⅢⅢ I	
Parrots	II	
Grass snakes	I	

The table shows a tally of the number of pets owned by third year children.

Each mark represents 1 pet, ⅢⅢ represents 5 pets.

1 Copy the table and fill in the total numbers.

2 As there are eight different types of pet, draw the horizontal axis 16cm long so that each block will be 2cm wide.

There are more cats than any other pet so the tallest column will represent 43.

1cm represents 2 pets. Label both axes and give the graph a title.

3 Write three sentences about what the graph shows.

4 Make up three questions about the graph for your friends.

5 Choose other topics to investigate, collect the figures, make the tables and draw graphs of your results.

Pets owned by 3rd year pupils

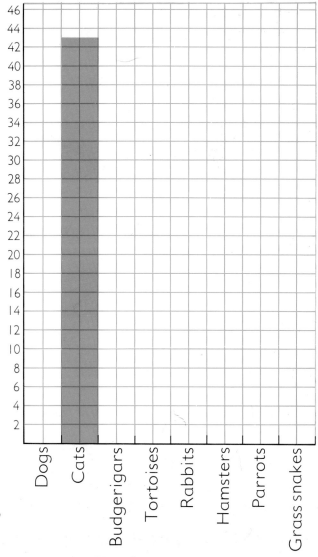

Temperature graphs

The following table gives the average maximum temperatures in °C for London.

Jan	Feb	Mar	Apl	May	June	July	Aug	Sept	Oct	Nov	Dec
6	7	10	13	17	20	22	21	19	14	10	7

These can be shown on a graph.

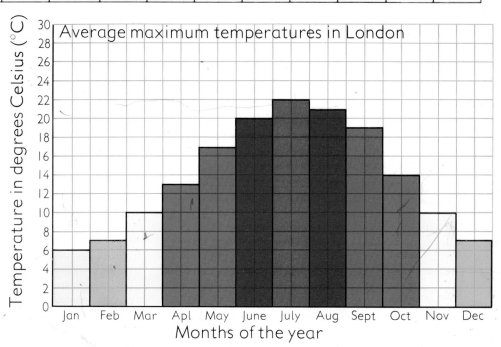

1 Which month had the highest temperature and which the lowest?
2 The difference between the highest and lowest temperatures is called the **range**. What is the range of temperatures in London?
3 Which months have the same temperatures?

A travel magazine gives the average maximum temperatures in °C for 3 Greek islands as:

	Jan	Feb	Mar	Apl	May	June	July	Aug	Sept	Oct	Nov	Dec
Limnos	11	12	13	18	23	27	30	30	26	22	16	13
Naxos	15	15	16	20	23	26	27	28	26	24	20	17
Zakynthos	14	14	16	20	25	29	32	32	29	25	20	16

4 Using a scale of 2cm for each month on the horizontal axis and 1cm for 2°C on the vertical axis, draw a separate graph for each island.

5 What is the range of temperatures for each island?

6 Which months in London are colder than the lowest month in Naxos?

7 How much warmer than London is Zakynthos in August?

Graphs of grouped data

Sometimes data (lists of figures) have to be arranged into groups before you draw a graph. For example, here is a list of the number of goals scored halfway through the football season by the teams in Division 1 of the English League:

| 32, | 28, | 14, | 8, | 15, | 22, | 22, | 24, | 39, | 20, |
| 20, | 24, | 26, | 25, | 23, | 21, | 14, | 35, | 26, | 19. |

1 a First, re-arrange them from the lowest number to the highest:
8, 14, 14, 15, 19, 20, 20, . . . and so on up to . . . 39.

b Then put them into groups, called *intervals*, of equal size.
Copy and complete this table:

Scores	1–5	6–10	11–15	16–20	21–25	26–30	31–35	36–40
Number of teams	0	1	3					1

c Now draw a graph with the number of goals along the horizontal axis and the number of teams on the vertical axis.

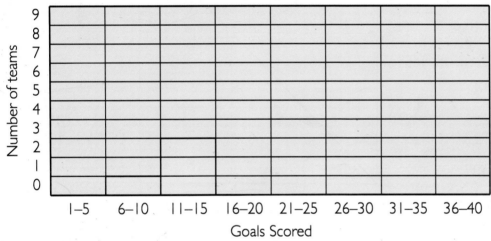

2 From your graph find how many teams scored:
a more than 25 goals, **b** less than 21 goals, **c** more than 15 goals.

3 a Here is a list of marks gained by 28 pupils for Test A.
Arrange the marks into equal intervals and plot a graph.

| 5 | 9 | 8 | 16 | 11 | 4 | 13 | 7 | 18 | 8 | 6 | 12 | 8 | 10 |
| 7 | 7 | 6 | 15 | 10 | 5 | 15 | 6 | 11 | 6 | 6 | 9 | 5 | 14 |

b These are the marks gained by the same 28 pupils for Test B.
Arrange these marks into equal intervals and plot a graph.

| 8 | 11 | 13 | 14 | 10 | 18 | 18 | 14 | 19 | 9 | 5 | 17 | 8 | 15 |
| 9 | 12 | 14 | 16 | 12 | 16 | 14 | 11 | 12 | 5 | 7 | 16 | 14 | 18 |

c Compare the two graphs. Which test do you think was easier? How can you tell?

Conversion graphs

In Britain the unit of currency is the pound (£). Other countries have different units of currency. In Upper Mathematica the unit of currency is the mult (mu). A visitor from Britain, last year, received 8mu for each £1.

The graph shows this conversion. The pounds have been marked on the horizontal axis and the mults on the vertical axis.

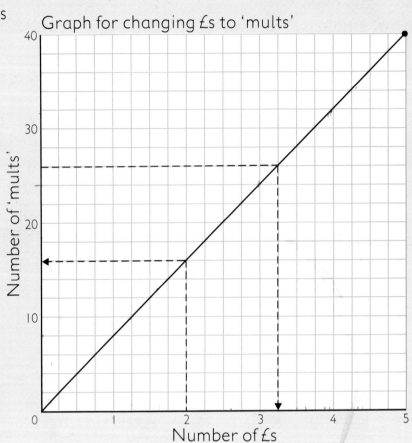

Graph for changing £s to 'mults'

1 How many squares are there for each £1?

2 How much is each square worth?

3 How many squares are there for ten mults?

4 How many mults is each square worth?

The broken line shows how to change £2 to mults. From £2 on the horizontal axis we go up to the conversion line and then read across to the mults column. £2 = 16mu.

To change 26mu to £ we follow the dotted line from 26mu across to the line and then down to the £ axis. 26mu = £3·25.

5 Convert these £ to mults:
  a £3   **c** £2·50   **e** £1·50   **g** £4·25
  b £5   **d** £3·50   **f** £3·75   **h** £2·75

6 Convert these mults to £:
  a 20mu   **c** 36mu   **e** 38mu   **g** 37mu
  b 30mu   **d** 42mu   **f** 46mu   **h** 25mu

Visitors to Upper Mathematica this year found that
they received 10 mults for £1.

1 Copy and complete:
  a £1 = 10mu   **c** £3 = ☐   **e** £5 = ☐
  b £2 = ☐   **d** £4 = ☐   **f** £0 = ☐

2 Draw axes as in the previous conversion graph but make the vertical
axis taller, taking it to 50 mults.

3 Plot the points in question 1 and join them with a straight line.

4 Using your graph, copy and complete this table:

£	1		4		1·50		2·75		4·75	
mults		30		50		35		$32\frac{1}{2}$		$37\frac{1}{2}$

To exchange larger amounts than £5 we can either say:
  £11 = £5+£5+£1 = 50mu+50mu+10mu = 110mu
or £18 = 6×£3   = 6×30mu   = 180mu

5 Using your graph copy, complete this table:

£	7	9	13	15	24	30
Mults						

6 Last year I bought a map in Upper Mathematica for 12mu.
How many £ was that? (Use last year's graph!)

7 This year it is still 12mu. What would I have saved in £ if I had bought it
this year?

8 A meal cost me 32mu last year. If the price is still the same this year
what do I save in £ if I have a similar meal?

9 When I went to Upper Mathematica last year my holiday cost me 1856
mults. How many pounds was equal to that amount?
If my holiday this year will cost the same number of mults how many
pounds will it cost?
What amount (in pounds) do I save this year?

A different sort of graph—a nomograph

This graph is designed to help us
to add or subtract.

1 On centimetre squared paper
draw three vertical lines each
20cm long and 3cm apart.
Letter them **A**, **B** and **C**.

2 Number them as in the diagram
with 2cm for each unit on the **A**
and **C** columns and 1cm for each
unit on the **B** column.

3 To add 5 and 4 place a ruler
across the chart (see diagram)
from 5 in column **A** to 4
in column **C**. The answer 9 is
in the middle column.

4 Use the nomogram to complete:

a $1+2=$	**f** $4\frac{1}{2}+3\frac{1}{2}=$
b $3+5=$	**g** $7+2\frac{1}{2}=$
c $7+2=$	**h** $3\frac{1}{2}+5=$
d $3\frac{1}{2}+2\frac{1}{2}=$	**i** $6\frac{1}{2}+1=$
e $6\frac{1}{2}+\frac{1}{2}=$	**j** $5\frac{1}{2}+2\frac{1}{2}=$

5 Look at the broken line.
Can you see how we could read
$9-5=4$?
Which column is the answer in?

6 Complete using the nomogram:

a $7-5=$	**e** $8\frac{1}{2}-3\frac{1}{2}=$
b $8-2=$	**f** $6\frac{1}{2}-5\frac{1}{2}=$
c $6-4=$	**g** $8-3\frac{1}{2}=$
d $7\frac{1}{2}-2\frac{1}{2}=$	**h** $6\frac{1}{2}-4=$

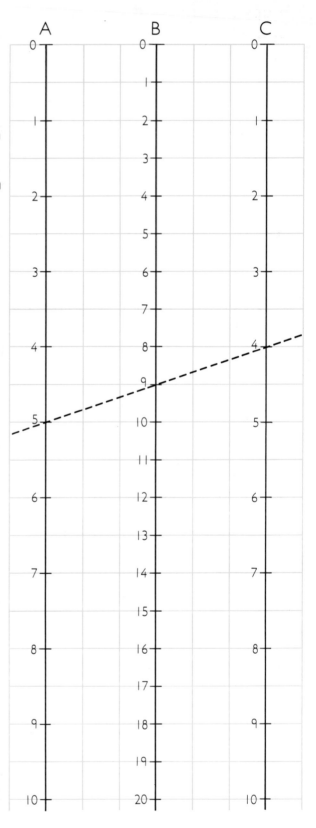

Chapter 16: Multiplication 2

Multiplication by 10 and 100

1 Copy and complete

    a $4 \times 10 =$ **c** $8 \times 10 =$ **e** $6 \times 10 =$ **g** $7 \times 10 =$

    b $3 \times 10 =$ **d** $5 \times 10 =$ **f** $9 \times 10 =$ **h** $10 \times 10 =$

To multiply a number by 10: move the digits **one** column to the left and put a zero in the empty units space.	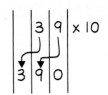

2 **a** $12 \times 10 =$ **d** $19 \times 10 =$ **g** $60 \times 10 =$ **j** $100 \times 10 =$

    b $15 \times 10 =$ **e** $26 \times 10 =$ **h** $91 \times 10 =$ **k** $130 \times 10 =$

    c $21 \times 10 =$ **f** $40 \times 10 =$ **i** $203 \times 10 =$ **l** $700 \times 10 =$

To multiply by multiples of 10 (20, 30, 40, 50, . . . etc.)
first multiply the digits then use the rule to multiply by 10.

$8 \times 40 = \quad 8 \times 4 \times 10$ $63 \times 20 = \quad 63 \times 2 \times 10$

$\quad\quad = \quad 32 \times 10 \longleftarrow$ 1st step $= 126 \times 10 \longleftarrow$ 1st step

$\quad\quad = \quad 320 \quad\longleftarrow$ 2nd step $= 1260 \quad\longleftarrow$ 2nd step

3 **a** 4×20 **d** 12×30 **g** 32×70 **j** 30×20

    b 7×50 **e** 14×60 **h** 46×50 **k** 40×40

    c 8×90 **f** 24×40 **i** 87×30 **l** 80×70

To multiply a number by 100: move the digits **two** columns to the left and put zeros in the empty units and tens columns.	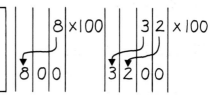

4 **a** 4×100 **c** 13×100 **e** 23×100 **g** 40×100

    b 6×100 **d** 27×100 **f** 89×100 **h** 70×100

To multiply by multiples of 100 (200, 300, 400, . . . etc.)
first multiply the digits then use the rule to multiply by 100.

5 **a** 4×200 **c** 13×400 **e** 23×600 **g** 29×700

    b 7×500 **d** 32×800 **f** 41×500 **h** 95×200

Here is a diagram which shows 16 × 14

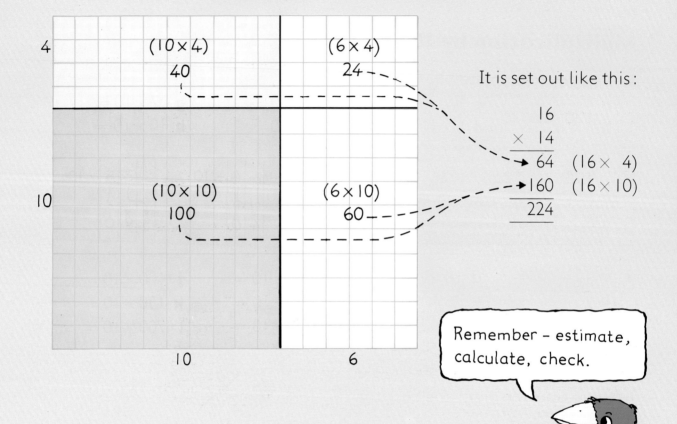

4   (10 × 4)   (6 × 4)
     40   24

It is set out like this:

```
     16
   ×  14
     64   (16 × 4)
    160   (16 × 10)
    224
```

10   (10 × 10)   (6 × 10)
     100   60

     10   6

Remember – estimate, calculate, check.

Do these in the same way. Draw a diagram for each and set it out like the example.

1
a	13	b	14	c	15	d	16	e	19
	×12		×13		×12		×15		×18

2 Try to do these without a diagram. The first is done for you.

a
```
     14
   × 12
     28   (14 × 2)
    140   (14 × 10)
    168
```

c	15	e	18	g	16	i	18
	×13		×13		×14		×16

b	15	d	14	f	16	h	17	j	19
	×14		×14		×16		×16		×19

This diagram shows 38×27

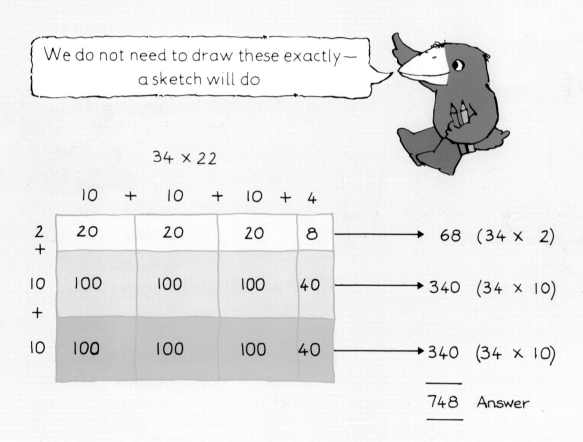

	10 +	10 +	10 +	8	
7 +	70	70	70	56	→ 266 (38 × 7)
10 +	100	100	100	80	→ 380 (38 × 10)
10	100	100	100	80	→ 380 (38 × 10)
					1026 Answer

We do not need to draw these exactly —
a sketch will do

34×22

	10 +	10 +	10 +	4	
2 +	20	20	20	8	→ 68 (34 × 2)
10 +	100	100	100	40	→ 340 (34 × 10)
10	100	100	100	40	→ 340 (34 × 10)
					748 Answer

1 Do these in the same way:
Remember — estimate, calculate, check.

a 23×17 **d** 25×23 **g** 52×37 **j** 58×51

b 45×14 **e** 29×21 **h** 46×34 **k** 69×62

c 37×19 **f** 46×28 **i** 62×43 **l** 78×59

Here is a plan divided into fewer parts. It shows 37×26.

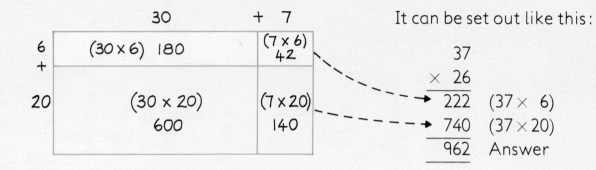

	30	+ 7
6 +	(30 × 6) 180	(7 × 6) 42
20	(30 × 20) 600	(7 × 20) 140

It can be set out like this:

```
        37
      × 26
       222   (37 × 6)
       740   (37 × 20)
       962   Answer
```

1 Do these in the same way:

    a 34×24 **b** 39×26 **c** 59×52 **d** 79×63

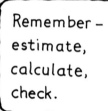

Remember –
estimate,
calculate,
check.

2 Try these without a diagram. The first is done for you.

```
a        43
       ×  37
         301   (43 × 7)
        1290   (43 × 30)
        1591
```

    b 47×33 **g** 85×64
    c 67×56 **h** 65×39
    d 29×29 **i** 94×87
    e 53×34 **j** 75×42
    f 73×59 **k** 93×34

3 **a** If there are 28 children in each class, how many will there be in 16 classes?

    b The seats for a concert are set out in rows of 32. If there is room for 18 rows, how many tickets can be sold?

    c What is the product of 43 and 27?

    d John's friends promise to give him 35p for every length he completes in a sponsored swim. If he swims 22 lengths, how much money should he receive?

    e How many nails will be needed to make 24 geoboards if there are 36 nails in each?

    f Find the floor area in m² of a rectangular hall which is 29m long and 21m wide.

    g 1, 4, 9, 16, 25, 36, 49, 64, 81 and 100 are the first 10 square numbers. Work out the next 10 square numbers up to 400. Check your result by studying the pattern.

    h Start by working out 35×35, then 36×34, then 37×33, then 38×32, and so on. Look for the pattern made by the products.

Chapter 17: Shape 2

Quadrilaterals

A quadrilateral is a four-sided figure.

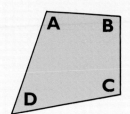

1   Draw any quadrilateral on a piece of paper
    and mark its angles **A**, **B**, **C**, **D** as in the diagram.
    Cut it out.

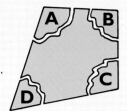

2   Tear off the four angles as shown.

3   Fit them together like this:

> The four angles
> of a quadrilateral
> add up to 360°.

4   Calculate the size, in degrees, of the lettered angles
    in these quadrilaterals.

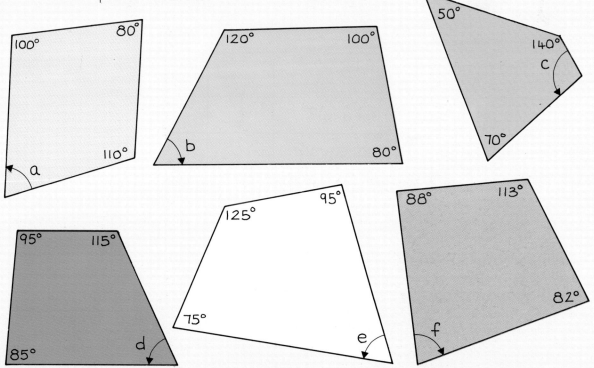

Some special quadrilaterals

Copy these quadrilaterals on to centimetre-squared paper.
Draw in the diagonals as in the diagram.
Cut out the shapes.

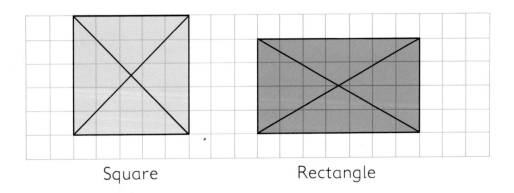

Square　　　　　　　　Rectangle

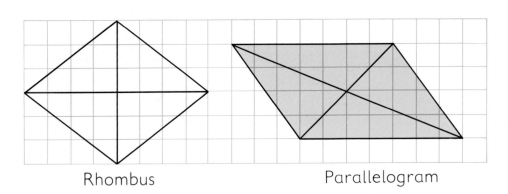

Rhombus　　　　　　　Parallelogram

1 Copy and complete this table:

	Square	Rhombus	Rectangle	Parallel-ogram
Four sides of a quadrilateral equal?			No	
Four angles of a quadrilateral equal?	Yes			
Diagonals same length?		No		
Do diagonals cut each other in half?				
Do diagonals cross at right angles?				
Are diagonals axes of symmetry?				
Are the angles of the quadrilateral cut in half by the diagonals?	Yes			

1 Copy these shapes carefully on to squared paper.

Mark all right angles like this:

Mark angles which are equal in the same colour:

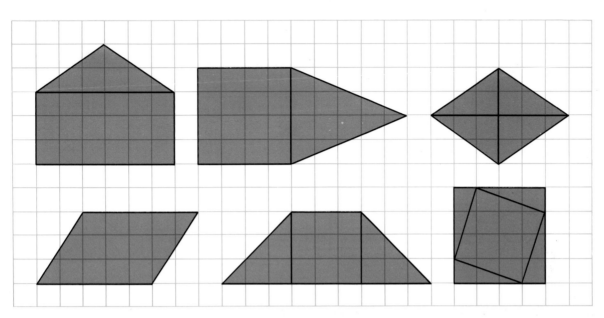

2 Find the size of each lettered angle in these diagrams:

Where lines are marked it means they are equal.

Remember: the 3 angles of a triangle together make 180°.

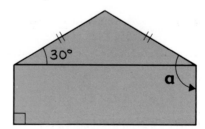

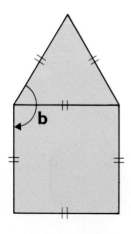

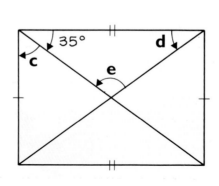

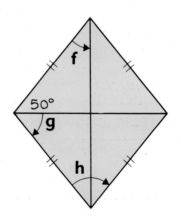

Tessellation

Some shapes fit together without gaps between them.
This is called tessellation. (The Latin word *tessella* means a tile.)
Look around for floors, walls or pathways that are covered
by tiles or slabs.

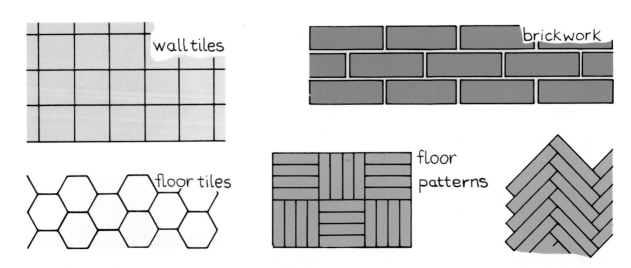

Cut out some 'tiles' from card or sticky paper, making sure the tiles in each
set are of the same shape and size.
You may have plastic shapes you can use.

Try sets of (**a**) equilateral, (**b**) right-angled, (**c**) scalene triangles
to see if they tessellate.

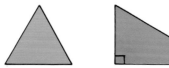

Squares and rectangles tessellate.
Now try other quadrilaterals
to see if they tessellate.

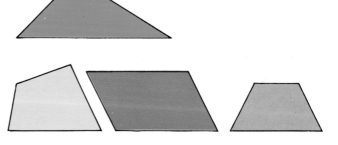

If 3 different colours are used,
the tessellation pattern of
a rhombus can be made to look
as though it is formed by cubes.
Try this for yourself.

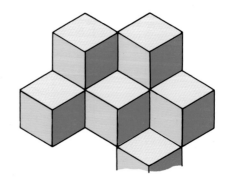

Symmetry of 2-D and 3-D shapes.

Plane shapes have two dimensions, length and width. Some plane shapes have lines of symmetry.

I   Draw these plane shapes and mark in any lines of symmetry:

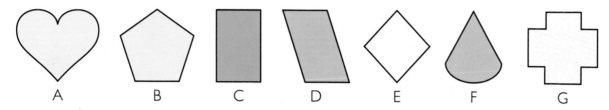

A   B   C   D   E   F   G

2   Which of these shapes have:
    a more than one line of symmetry?   **b** rotational symmetry?
    c Which one has rotational symmetry but **not** line symmetry?

Solid or 3-dimensional shapes have length, width and thickness or height. Some of them may be symmetrical—these will have a **plane of symmetry**.
If a solid is cut through its plane of symmetry and a mirror is placed up to the cut surface, the mirror image makes the solid look whole again.

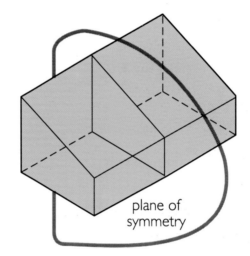

plane of symmetry

3   How many planes of symmetry does a cuboid have?
Make a cuboid from Plasticine and cut through the planes.

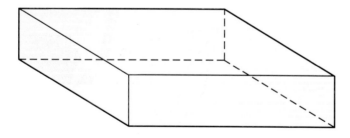

4   Use cubes and a piece of card to make a symmetrical shape. The part of the shape on one side of the card must be the mirror image of the part on the other side.

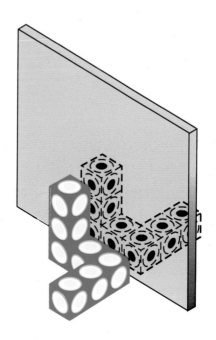

The diagram shows two ways a wooden floor tile
may fit into place, ... like this . . or like this.
But it could be turned over to fit
two more ways. This floor tile has
an order of symmetry of 4.

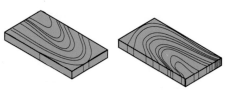

1 What is the order of symmetry of a
floor tile with a square face?

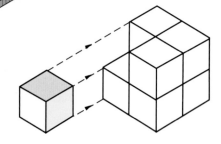

2 A cube building block will fit into
this space. How many ways will it fit?
Use some cubes to find out. It helps if
you chalk each face of the single cube a
different colour.

3 Soften a large ball of Plasticine in your hands.

Take a wooden or plastic square based pyramid and cover the sloping triangular sides with a thin smear of Vaseline.

Push the Plasticine down over the point of the pyramid and press in the sides to hold the pyramid firmly.

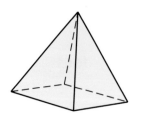
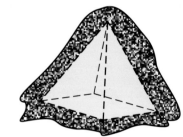

Slide the pyramid out from the
Plasticine leaving a cavity.
How many different ways can the
pyramid be placed back in the cavity?

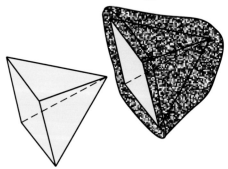

4 Try the same experiment but this time use a regular tetrahedron—
that is a triangular based pyramid with
all four faces the same shape and size.
How many different ways can this fit
into its cavity?

Chapter 18: Division 2

In Chapter 16 we learned how to multiply by ten and multiples of ten.

To multiply by 100 we move digits
2 columns to the left and fill
the tens and units spaces with zeros.

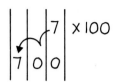
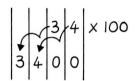

1 Copy and complete these:

a $4 \times 100 =$ **c** $12 \times 100 =$ **e** $39 \times 100 =$ **g** $73 \times 100 =$

b $9 \times 100 =$ **d** $27 \times 100 =$ **f** $48 \times 100 =$ **h** $86 \times 100 =$

Multiplication by multiples of 100 is carried out in two steps:
For example: 34×600

$$34 \times 6 \times 100$$
$$204 \times 100$$
$$20400$$

Multiply first by the six, then by the hundred.

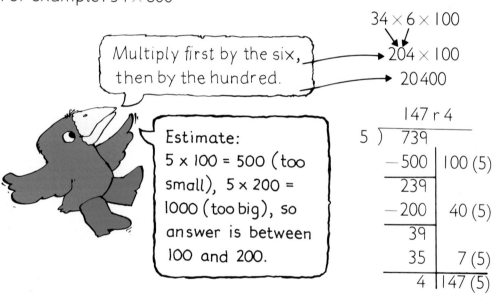

Estimate:
$5 \times 100 = 500$ (too small), $5 \times 200 = 1000$ (too big), so answer is between 100 and 200.

```
      147 r 4
5 ) 739
   -500 | 100 (5)
    239
   -200 | 40 (5)
     39
     35 | 7 (5)
      4 | 147 (5)
```

2 Copy and complete these:

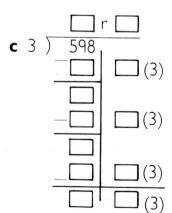

a $4) \overline{536}$
```
   -400 | ☐ (4)
    136
   -☐  | 30 (4)
    16
   -☐  | ☐ (4)
        | ☐ (4)
```

b $6) \overline{893}$ ☐ r ☐
```
   -☐  | 100 (6)
    293
   -☐  | 40 (6)
    ☐
   -☐  | ☐ (6)
    ☐  | ☐ (6)
```

c $3) \overline{598}$ ☐ r ☐
```
   -☐  | ☐ (3)
    ☐
   -☐  | ☐ (3)
    ☐
   -☐  | ☐ (3)
    ☐  | ☐ (3)
```

I Do these the same way—estimate first:

a $376 \div 2$ c $671 \div 5$ e $831 \div 7$ g $975 \div 8$

b $439 \div 3$ d $624 \div 4$ f $846 \div 6$ h $981 \div 9$

Estimate: 3 × 200 = 600 (too small), 3 × 300 = 900 (too big), so answer is between 200 and 300.

```
              279 r 2
    3 ) 839
       -600 | 200  (3)
        239
       -210 |  70  (3)
         29
       - 27 |   9  (3)
          2 | 279  (3)
```

2 Copy and complete these:

```
        □                    □                    □
a 4 )  936          b 2 )   947          c 3 )   834
   -  □   □ (4)        - 800  □ (2)          - □   □ (3)
      □                   147                  □
   - 120  □ (4)        -  □   □ (2)          - □   □ (3)
      □                   □                    □
   -  16  □ (4)        -  □   □ (2)          - □   □ (3)
          □ (4)           □   □ (2)                □ (3)
```

d $749 \div 3$ f $826 \div 2$ h $713 \div 2$ j $874 \div 3$

e $911 \div 4$ g $630 \div 3$ i $981 \div 4$ k $999 \div 4$

Dividing by numbers greater than 10

The same method can be used to divide by larger numbers.

```
               15 r I
   13 )  196
        -130 | 10 (13)
          66
        - 65 |  5 (13)
           I | 15 (13)
```

1 Copy and complete

a 15) 193 ☐ r ☐
   − ☐ 10 (15)
   ☐
   − 30 ☐ (15)
   ☐ ☐ (15)

b 17) 218 ☐ r ☐
   − ☐ 10 (17)
   48
   − ☐ ☐ (17)
   ☐ ☐ (17)

c 18) 222 ☐ r ☐
   − ☐ ☐ (18)
   ☐
   − ☐ ☐ (18)
   ☐ ☐ (18)

d $173 \div 14$ **f** $185 \div 15$ **h** $172 \div 13$ **j** $216 \div 18$
e $198 \div 16$ **g** $203 \div 17$ **i** $221 \div 19$ **k** $292 \div 17$

Estimate first. Then, if you use multiples of 10, it shortens the work.

```
         25 r 7
17 )  432
    −340 | 20 (17)
      92 |
    − 85 |  5 (17)
       7 | 25 (17)
```

2 Do these the same way :

a $312 \div 13$ **c** $321 \div 12$ **e** $765 \div 15$ **g** $816 \div 19$
b $477 \div 15$ **d** $414 \div 14$ **f** $552 \div 17$ **h** $937 \div 18$

3 a John has 408 stamps. He sticks them on 17 pages of his album.
   If there are the same number on each page, how many stamps are
   there on a page?

b In a school 392 children are equally divided into 14 classes.
   How many are there in each class?

c In the class library each shelf, on average, holds 18 books.
   How many shelves will be needed for 432 books?

d Fifteen biscuits make one packet. How many packets can be made
   from 476 biscuits? How many are left?

e How many perfume bottles, each holding 16 millilitres, can be filled
   from a $\frac{1}{2}$-litre container?

Chapter 19: Time

The 24-hour clock

The clock shows half-past eight or 8.30. To make sure
people know if we mean morning or evening, we have
to say a.m. (before noon) or p.m. (after noon).
As there are 24 hours in a day, if we use the 24-hour
system for telling the time we do not have to say
a.m. or p.m.

8.30 a.m. is 08.30   8.30 p.m. is 20.30

Notice that each number on the inner ring (the p.m.
part) is 12 more than the number in the outer ring.
6 a.m. is 06.00   but 6 p.m. is 18.00.
11.15 a.m. is 11.15 but 11.15 p.m. is 23.15.

1 Use a strip of squared paper to make a 'time line' like this:

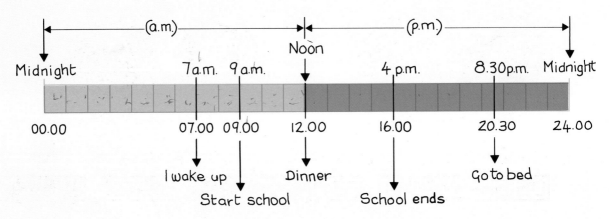

Mark in some special times of the day using both a.m./p.m. and 24-hour
systems.

2 Write these times using the 24-hour system. Always use two figures for
the hours (01, 02, 03, . . . 09, 10, 11, . . . 23, 24) and two figures for the
minutes (00 . . . 59).

a 1 a.m.	**e** 5 p.m.	**i** 10.25 p.m.	**m** 1 minute to midnight
b 1 p.m.	**f** midnight	**j** 8.45 p.m.	**n** 1 minute past midnight
c noon	**g** 9.30 p.m.	**k** 2.35 p.m.	**o** 5 past noon
d 5 a.m.	**h** 10.15 a.m.	**l** 5 past 3 p.m.	**p** 10 to 3 p.m.

From one time to another

Working out how long from 9.15 a.m. to 4.25 p.m., for example,
is much easier using the 24-hour system.

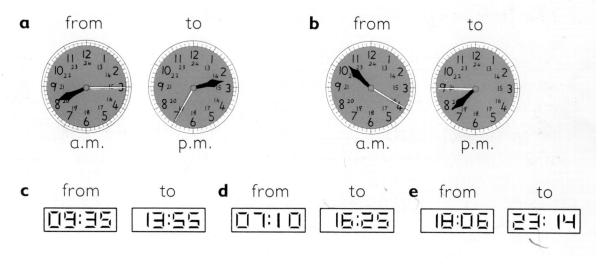

Using the 12-hour system:
from 9.15 a.m. to 10 a.m. is
from 10 a.m. to noon is
from noon to 4.25 p.m. is

h	min
	45
2	
4	25
6	70	= 7h 10min.

Using the 24-hour system

h	min
16	25
−09	15
7	10

1 Use the 24-hour system to find how long between times shown by
   the two clock faces or digital displays:

a   from   to   **b**   from   to

a.m.   p.m.   a.m.   p.m.

c   from   to   **d**   from   to   **e**   from   to

09:35   13:55   07:10   16:25   18:06   23:14

2 **a** Anne starts school at 09.15 and finishes at 15.45.
       How many hours and minutes is she at school?
   b If she has $1\frac{1}{4}$ hours for dinner time and two play-times of 15 minutes
       each, how much time is there for lessons?

3 **a** A marathon race started at 14.05 and the winner crossed the
       finishing line at 19.53. How long did he take?
   b The second runner came in 12 minutes later.
       At what time did he finish?

Train, bus and airway timetables are printed in the 24-hour system. They do not have to print a.m. or p.m. hundreds of times.

1 Work out the time taken for each of these journeys:

	depart	arrive
a	11.00	15.00
b	08.00	09.30
c	16.00	23.00

	depart	arrive
d	01.00	18.00
e	05.00	14.30
f	06.30	12.45

	depart	arrive
g	14.15	19.28
h	09.32	13.48
i	07.10	07.37

If there are 'not enough' minutes for a subtraction, exchange 1 hour for 60 minutes.

16.20 becomes 15h and 80mins.

$$\begin{array}{r} 15.80 \\ - 11.50 \\ \hline 4.30 \end{array}$$

2 Change these times to the 24-hour system and find the time taken for each journey:

	depart	arrive
a	10.15 a.m.	5 p.m.
b	5.30 a.m.	noon
c	11.45 a.m.	9.15 p.m.

	depart	arrive
d	8.35 a.m.	9.10 a.m.
e	8.35 a.m.	9.10 p.m.
f	6.50 a.m.	1.15 p.m.

	depart	arrive
g	3.48 a.m.	1.40 p.m.
h	5.55 p.m.	9.12 p.m.
i	7.32 a.m.	5.10 p.m.

Sometimes the full stop between hours and minutes is missed out, so that a railway timetable looks like this:

Exeter Central	0639	0758	1352	1642	2253
Topsham	0651	0815	1404	1655	2305
Exton	0655	0819	1408	1659	2309
Commando Camp	0657	0821	1410	1701	2311
Exmouth	0704	0828	1417	1708	2318

3 a Do the trains all take the same time over each part of the journey?
 b List the time taken from each station to the next by the 2253 train from Exeter Central.
 c At what time does the slowest train leave Exeter Central?
 d If you arrive at Topsham at half-past three in the afternoon, how long will you have to wait for the next train to Exmouth?
 e What is the time of the latest train you can catch from Exeter Central to be sure of getting to Exmouth by 6 p.m.?

4 Make a timetable of your own for journeys from Exmouth to Exeter Central.

Multiplication of time

John's father works 7 hours 15 minutes a day.
How many hours and minutes does he work in a 5-day week?

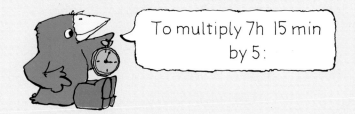

To multiply 7h 15 min
by 5:

Set out the hours and minutes in
separate columns like this:

Multiply the 15 min by 5 and write
the answer, 75 mins, below the answer line.

75 min = (60 min + 15 min) = 1h 15 min

Write 15 in the minutes column and
the small 1 under the hours column.

7h × 5 = 35h. Add on the 1h to make 36h.

	h	min
	7	15
×		5
	36	15
	1	75

1 Set these out in the same way:
   a 2h 25 min × 3   **d** 3h 10 min × 9   **g** 8h 45 min × 7
   b 4h 15 min × 4   **e** 6h 12 min × 5   **h** 4h 52 min × 4
   c 8h 5 min × 8   **f** 7h 22 min × 6   **i** 9h 58 min × 8

2 A school's heating is switched on at 08.30 and switched off at 15.10
   each day.
   a How long is the heating on each day?
   b How long is the heating on in a 5-day week?

3 A nurse is on duty from 12.10 to 20.00 each day for 6 days.
   How many hours is this?

4 The night-duty nurse starts at 20.00 and comes off duty at 06.15
   the next day.
   a How long is this?
   b How many hours duty will a night nurse do in 6 nights?

Chapter 20: Fractions 2

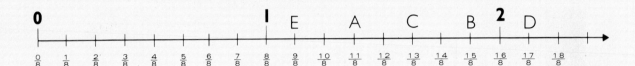

Along the top this number line shows 0, 1 and 2. Below the line it is marked in eighths. Point A can be described in two ways —at the top it is $1\frac{3}{8}$ and at the bottom $\frac{11}{8}$.

1 Describe points B, C, D, E in the same way.

Numbers which are whole numbers and fractions, like $1\frac{3}{8}$ and $2\frac{1}{8}$ are **mixed numbers**.

Numbers which have larger numerators than denominators like $\frac{11}{8}$ and $\frac{19}{8}$ are **improper fractions**.

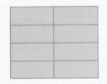  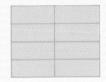 

2 This diagram shows the mixed number $3\frac{3}{8}$.
Each whole one is $\frac{8}{8}$ so altogether $3(\frac{8}{8})+\frac{3}{8}=\frac{24}{8}+\frac{3}{8}=\frac{27}{8}$

Copy and complete :

a $1\frac{4}{5}=\frac{\square}{5}$ d $3\frac{1}{4}=\frac{\square}{4}$ g $3\frac{4}{5}=\frac{\square}{5}$ j $4\frac{7}{8}=\frac{\square}{8}$

b $2\frac{2}{3}=\frac{\square}{3}$ e $3\frac{2}{3}=\frac{\square}{3}$ h $4\frac{1}{4}=\frac{\square}{4}$ k $5\frac{7}{10}=\frac{\square}{10}$

c $2\frac{4}{5}=\frac{\square}{5}$ f $2\frac{7}{8}=\frac{\square}{8}$ i $4\frac{2}{3}=\frac{\square}{3}$ l $6\frac{2}{3}=\frac{\square}{3}$

Change $\frac{11}{4}$ to a mixed number.
Each whole number will be $\frac{4}{4}$
so $\frac{11}{4}=2\frac{3}{4}$.

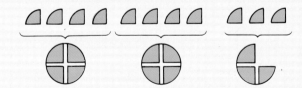

3 Change to mixed numbers :

a $\frac{7}{2}$ d $\frac{19}{4}$ g $\frac{27}{8}$ j $\frac{64}{9}$

b $\frac{14}{3}$ e $\frac{27}{5}$ h $\frac{41}{10}$ k $\frac{55}{8}$

c $\frac{13}{5}$ f $\frac{25}{6}$ i $\frac{43}{8}$ l $\frac{76}{9}$

Addition of mixed numbers

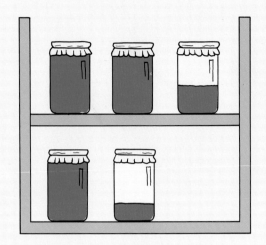

If there are $2\frac{1}{2}$ jars of jam on the top shelf and $1\frac{1}{3}$ jars on the bottom shelf, how much jam is there altogether?

(There are 3 full jars.)
(change $\frac{1}{2}$ and $\frac{1}{3}$ into sixths.)

$2\frac{1}{2}+1\frac{1}{3}$
$3+\frac{1}{2}+\frac{1}{3}$
$3+\frac{3}{6}+\frac{2}{6}$
$3\frac{5}{6}$

1 Do these in the same way:

a $3\frac{1}{4}+1\frac{1}{3}$ **c** $4\frac{2}{5}+1\frac{1}{3}$ **e** $3\frac{2}{3}+4\frac{1}{8}$ **g** $2\frac{2}{3}+3\frac{1}{8}$

b $2\frac{1}{2}+3\frac{3}{10}$ **d** $3\frac{2}{5}+1\frac{1}{4}$ **f** $2\frac{3}{10}+3\frac{1}{4}$ **h** $4\frac{1}{6}+2\frac{3}{4}$

Add $4\frac{2}{3}+3\frac{3}{5} = 7+\frac{10}{15}+\frac{9}{15}$

$= 7\frac{19}{15}$

$= 7+1\frac{4}{15}$

$= 8\frac{4}{15}$

This is an improper fraction and $\frac{19}{15}=1\frac{4}{15}$.

2 Do these in the same way:

a $2\frac{2}{3}+3\frac{3}{4}$ **d** $4\frac{3}{4}+2\frac{2}{5}$ **g** $3\frac{2}{3}+2\frac{4}{5}$ **j** $2\frac{7}{8}+4\frac{3}{5}$

b $1\frac{1}{2}+3\frac{3}{5}$ **e** $1\frac{3}{8}+4\frac{2}{3}$ **h** $2\frac{3}{4}+5\frac{7}{12}$ **k** $3\frac{7}{9}+3\frac{1}{4}$

c $2\frac{3}{8}+1\frac{2}{3}$ **f** $5\frac{7}{10}+3\frac{3}{4}$ **i** $1\frac{5}{8}+4\frac{2}{3}$ **l** $4\frac{5}{8}+5\frac{7}{10}$

Subtraction of mixed numbers

If there are $3\frac{1}{2}$ cakes on the table
how can we take $1\frac{2}{3}$ away?

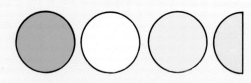 $3\frac{1}{2} - 1\frac{2}{3}$

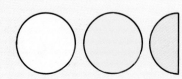 $2\frac{1}{2} - \frac{2}{3}$

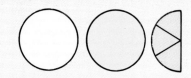 $= 2\frac{3}{6} - \frac{4}{6}$

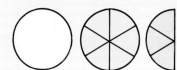 $= 1\frac{9}{6} - \frac{4}{6}$

$= 1\frac{5}{6}$

I can take 1 away.

Change $\frac{1}{2}$ and $\frac{2}{3}$ into sixths.

There are not enough sixths to take $\frac{4}{6}$ away so I must change one of my whole ones into sixths.

1 Do these in the same way:

a $3\frac{1}{2} - 1\frac{3}{4}$ d $4\frac{1}{5} - 2\frac{1}{4}$ g $5\frac{1}{2} - 3\frac{3}{5}$ j $6\frac{4}{9} - 5\frac{1}{2}$

b $4\frac{1}{3} - 2\frac{1}{2}$ e $4\frac{2}{3} - 1\frac{4}{5}$ h $6\frac{1}{2} - 4\frac{5}{6}$ k $4\frac{5}{9} - 2\frac{3}{4}$

c $5\frac{2}{3} - 3\frac{7}{8}$ f $6\frac{3}{8} - 4\frac{2}{3}$ i $5\frac{2}{5} - 1\frac{2}{3}$ l $4\frac{2}{3} - 3\frac{7}{8}$

Chapter 21: Length 2

Measuring in millimetres

This ruler, marked in millimetres (mm) is used to measure
the length of a paper clip.

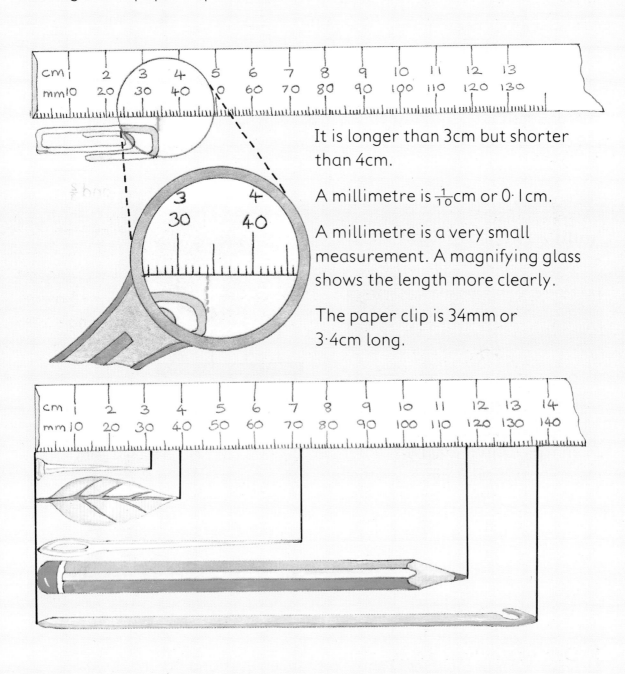

It is longer than 3cm but shorter
than 4cm.

A millimetre is $\frac{1}{10}$cm or 0·1cm.

A millimetre is a very small
measurement. A magnifying glass
shows the length more clearly.

The paper clip is 34mm or
3·4cm long.

I Record the length first in millimetres then in centimetres of:
   a the pin   **c** the needle   **e** the crochet hook
   b the leaf   **d** the pencil

Remember: there are 10 millimetres (mm) in 1 centimetre (cm)
so $1mm = \frac{1}{10}cm = 0.1cm$.

1 a ☐ mm = 2cm   e 80mm = ☐ cm   i ☐ mm = 9·2cm
   b ☐ mm = 7cm   f 85mm = ☐ cm   j ☐ mm = 0·1cm
   c ☐ mm = 0·7cm   g   3mm = ☐ cm   k 120mm = ☐ cm
   d 30mm = ☐ cm   h 100mm = ☐ cm   l 135mm = ☐ cm

10 millimetres = 1 centimetre
100 centimetres = 1 metre   }   1000 millimetres = 1 metre

'milli' comes from a Latin word
meaning a 'thousand'.

$1mm = \frac{1}{1000}m = 0.001m$

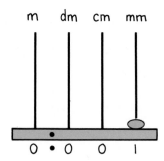

285mm = 200mm + 80mm + 5mm
     = 20cm + 8cm + 5mm
     =   2dm + 8cm + 5mm
     = 0·2m   + 0·08m + 0·005m
     = 0·285m

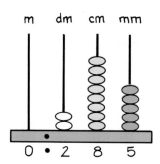

2 Draw abacus pictures of these measurements and record them
   in metres:

   a 346mm   c 307mm   e 80mm   g 990mm   i 1234mm
   b 520mm   d 25mm   f 6mm   h 1000mm   j 1050mm

1 a Use a ruler marked in mm to check these measurements.
Make sure the zero is level with the end of the line.

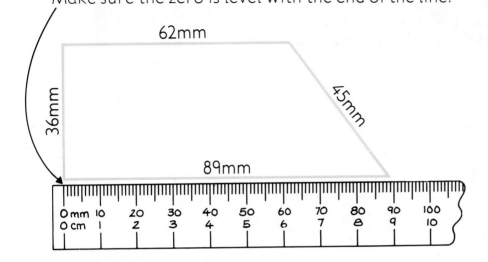

b Estimate the perimeter of this shape
c Work out the perimeter and record it first in mm then in m.

2 Measure the sides of these shapes in millimetres.
Estimate and then work out the perimeter of each shape.
Record in mm and m.

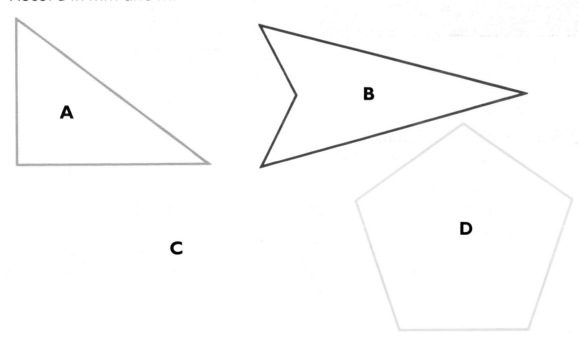

3 a Write down the names of the shapes in question 2.
b What is the difference between the longest and shortest perimeters?
c What is the quicker way of working out the perimeter of **D**?

To find the perimeter of
a regular octagon with sides
129mm long, multiply 129mm × 8.
(Estimate first:
129mm × 8 ≃ 130mm × 8 = 1040mm)
Perimeter is 1032mm or 1·032 metres.

```
      129              or      129
    ×   8                    ×   8
     72 (  9 × 8)            1032
    160 ( 20 × 8)             27
    800 (100 × 8)
   1032
```

1 If a regular octagon has a perimeter of 1 metre,
   what is the length of a side in mm?

2 Estimate and then work out the perimeter of a regular
   hexagon whose sides are 172mm long.

This graph paper is marked in
centimetre and 2-millimetre squares.
The side of each small square
is 2mm long.

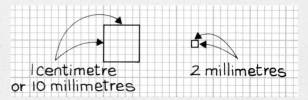

1 centimetre
or 10 millimetres   2 millimetres

3 Spread out your hand first on a strip of graph paper. Carefully mark
   where the tips of your thumb and little finger come and measure your
   hand-span as accurately as you can in millimetres. Measure
   the hand-span in mm of some of your friends and draw a graph of them.

4 Is your left hand-span the same as your right hand-span?

5 Use 2-mm graph paper to measure accurately the diameters of different
   coins (10p, 5p, 2p, 1p, $\frac{1}{2}$p), the length and breadth of stamps and the
   lengths of screws, bolts, nails, etc.

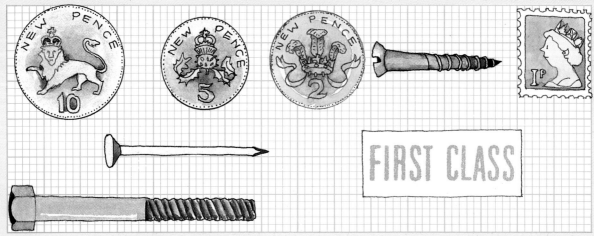

Chapter 22: Probability

Estimating probability

1 Toss up a coin several times.
Keep a tally of how many times it
lands 'heads' and how many times 'tails'.

	tally	total
Heads	~~IIII~~ ~~IIII~~ I	
Tails	~~IIII~~ ~~IIII~~ IIII	

There are two ways the coin can land—either 'heads' or 'tails'.
The chance of 'heads' turning up is 1 out of 2, so the **probability**
of a head is $\frac{1}{2}$.
The chance of 'tails' turning up is 1 out of 2, so the **probability** of a tail is
also $\frac{1}{2}$.
There is an **even chance** of a 'head' or a 'tail' turning up.
This can be shown as halfway along a **probability** scale:

Impossible No chance	Poor chance	Even chance	Good chance	Certain
0		$\frac{1}{2}$		1

When we say that the probability of tossing a 'head' is $\frac{1}{2}$ we do
not mean that **exactly** half the times it will land as 'heads'.
We mean it is **likely** that about half the times it is tossed the
coin will land as 'heads'.
For example, if you toss a coin 60 times it is **likely** you will get
approximately 30 'heads'.
30 is a **reasonable estimate** of the number of 'heads' you can expect.

2 Compare the result of your coin-tossing with the probable
result. How close was it? If it was not very close toss the coin
some more and add to your tally.

3 About how many heads do you expect if you toss a coin:
  a 50   **b** 80   **c** 1000   **d** 120 times?

4 About how many tails do you expect if you toss a coin:
  a 90   **b** 2000   **c** 100   **d** 101 times?

5 Write down some other events that have a probability of $\frac{1}{2}$.

1 Put 10 red, 10 yellow and 10 blue cubes
or counters in a bag.
Shake the bag and, without looking, take
one cube out.
Do this several times, putting the cube
back in the bag and shaking it each time.
Keep a tally of how many reds, yellows and
blues you choose.

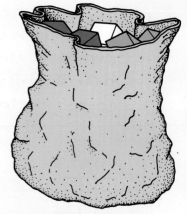

	Tally	Total
Red	卌 卌 ‖	
Yellow	卌 ‖‖‖	
Blue	卌 卌 卌	

There are 30 cubes in the bag and 10 of them are red so the
chance of picking a red cube is 10 out of 30.
The **probability** of picking a red is $\frac{10}{30}$ or $\frac{1}{3}$.
This is one-third of the way along the probability scale:

Impossible No chance		Poor chance	Even chance	Good chance		Certain
0		$\frac{1}{3}$	$\frac{1}{2}$			1

The **probability** of picking a yellow is $\frac{10}{30}$ or $\frac{1}{3}$ and the
probability of picking a blue is also $\frac{10}{30}$ or $\frac{1}{3}$.
Notice that the probability of choosing a green cube is 0
(impossible) and the probability of choosing a cube which is not
green is 1 (certain).

2 Compare the result of your colour choosing with the probable
result. How close was it? What can you do so that the two
results are likely to get closer?

3 Approximately how many red cubes do you expect if you pick out:
a 60　**b** 330　**c** 360　**d** 180 cubes?

4 Approximately how many blue cubes do you expect if you pick out:
a 99　**b** 3300　**c** 600　**d** 602 cubes?

5 Make up the rules of a dice game so that each of three players
has a probability of $\frac{1}{3}$ of winning.

1 Hold a shuffled pack of 52 cards face downwards. Turn over one card. Do this several times, replacing the card and shuffling the pack each time. Keep a tally of how many of each suit you choose.

	tally	total
Spades	卌 卌 ||	
Hearts	卌 |||	
Clubs	卌 ||	
Diamonds	卌 卌	

There are 52 cards in the pack and 13 of them are spades so the chance of choosing a spade is $\frac{13}{52}$ or $\frac{1}{4}$.
This is only a quarter of the way along the probability scale, so you have a **less than even** chance of choosing a spade.

Impossible No chance	Poor chance	Even chance	Good chance	Certain
0	$\frac{1}{4}$	$\frac{1}{2}$		1

2 What is the probability of turning over:
   a a heart   **b** a club   **c** a diamond   **d** a red card?

3 About how many spades do you expect if you choose a card:
   a 40   **b** 88   **c** 240   **d** 480 times?

4 Approximately how many clubs do you expect if you choose a card:
   a 200   **b** 120   **c** 320   **d** 321 times?

5 How close were your results in question **1** to the expected results? What can you do to make them closer?

6 There are 160 people in a hall and one lady stands up to make a speech.
   a What is the probability that she was born in a leap year?
   b How many of the people in the hall are likely to have been born in a leap year?

Rolling dice

1 When rolling an unbiased die, there is an equal chance that each of the six faces will finish on top.
The probability of a ⚀ is $\frac{1}{6}$.
The probability of a ⚁ is $\frac{1}{6}$,
and so on for each face.

1 a If you roll a die 30 times how many times would you expect a to be scored? Do it and record your result.

b If you roll a die 60 times how many times would you expect a to be scored? Do it and record your result.

c If you roll a die 90 times how many times would you expect a to be scored? Do it and record your result.

2 What do you notice about your results for questions **1a**, **b** and **c**?

The table reminds you of the 36 possible results from rolling two dice.
Five can be scored in 4 ways out of 36, so the probability of scoring five is $\frac{4}{36}$ or $\frac{1}{9}$.
Two can be scored in 1 way out of 36, so the probability of scoring two is $\frac{1}{36}$.

	1	2	3	4	5	6
1	2	3	4	5	6	7
2	3	4	5	6	7	8
3	4	5	6	7	8	9
4	5	6	7	8	9	10
5	6	7	8	9	10	11
6	7	8	9	10	11	12

3 What is the probability of scoring:
a twelve   **b** seven   **c** ten   **d** eight?

4 If you roll two dice 180 times how many times approximately would you expect to score: **a** seven   **b** nine   **c** four   **d** three?

5 It is impossible to score 13 with two dice so what is the probability of scoring 13?

6 What is the probability of scoring less than 13?

7 Draw a line 12 centimetres long and mark it like this as a probability scale:

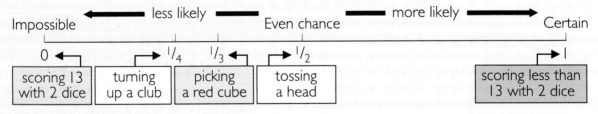

Mark on your scale your estimates of the probabilities of these events:
'I will see a dog on the way home', 'I will not see a dog on the way home',
'I will see a kangaroo on the way home', 'I shall watch TV to-night',
'I will make a spelling mistake today'. Make up some of your own.